TOO MUCH, NOT ENOUGH

You are enough!

Too Much, Not Enough:
A guide to decreasing anxiety and finding balance through intentional choices

By Tara Sanderson, PsyD, MBA

The concepts and conversations in this book have been set down to the best of the author's ability. Some names and details have been changed to protect the privacy of individuals. Any therapy sessions referred to included written permission from all participants.

First paperback edition September 2019

Edited by Paula Hampton, Ankeny Editing, www.ankenyediting.com
Design by Brandon Buerkle, Society of Fonts, www.societyoffonts.com
Author photograph by Bee España, Bee Joy Photography, www.bee-joy.com

ISBN 978-1-7331983-1-8 (paperback)
ISBN 978-1-7331983-0-1 (hardback)
ISBN 978-1-7331983-2-5 (ebook)

Published by
Tara Sanderson

www.drtarasanderson.com

Table of Contents

Acknowledgements

I am so grateful for the opportunity to write this book. I couldn't have done it without my husband, Stephen. You are the most kindhearted, generous, and loving man I have ever met. Your quirky Sanderisms, your heart to serve, and your love for me are unmeasurable. I am so blessed to have you in my life. You gave me so much of yourself while I wrote this book. You offered hard truths about my writing and provided wisdom throughout. Thank you. I love you.

Ashlee Kulpa, Amanda Greene, Katherine Merrill: I want to thank you for giving of your time to read my book and give me feedback (and courage) to get this published. Your encouragement, criticisms, and desire to see the best book I could write helped me to make my ideas a reality. I could not imagine life without your love, your support, and your friendship. I am honored to have you in my life.

Melanie Martin, you have been my *anam cara* (soul friend) since I was a young girl. Your thoughtfulness and passion have given me strength throughout my life.

Kristi Schmidlkofer, I couldn't believe you wanted to be my friend in Graduate School. I was sure that you were going to just be one of the cool kids that I wouldn't get a chance to know. You have been such a passionate friend. So kind and thoughtful. Our lives have been full of laughs, tears and margaritas. I am grateful to know you, and so blessed. Thank you for being there for me.

Mom, you have always believed in me. I know you have given everything to make sure that Sean and I knew that you loved us and wanted what was best for us. I am thankful to have known love like this. You imparted so many values and lessons that have formed me into who I am today. Thank you, I love you.

Daddy, you always introduce me with such pride in who I have become. I know that it is because of your belief in my ability to do amazing things that I have become who I am. Thank you for every opportunity you have supported and every ounce of love you have given me. I love you Daddy.

Grandma Elzora, you are such an amazing woman. Your love and understanding have been my rock. You have believed in me and you are one of my favorite people in the world.

Sean, you are my favorite brother. Thank you for always supporting me.

Susan and Shane Sanderson, I feel so loved in your family. You raised incredible kids and have always been so gracious to Stephen and me as we have gone through our life together. Thank you for all your support.

The rest of the Sandersons, thank you so much for welcoming me into your family. I have always felt valued and important. When I joined the family, I became a sister-in-law, an aunt, and a great aunt! (You know how much I love titles!)

Amanda Burt, Rebecca Karr, Dr. Degelman, Holly Hetrick, Kami Green, Elizabeth and Bryon Forbes, Jerri Pence, Marina Matthews, Susan and Micheal Skehen, Amanda and Mark Zimmerman, Cory Del Vilar, Janet Pettis, Brandon and Korie Buerkle, Bee and Col, Misha Moon, Kate Stidd and Richard Clark, Rebecca Karr, Morgan Gist MacDonald (and anyone else I have forgotten and will feel guilty about later): Thank you for being such an important part of my life and helping me become the person I am today.

I also want to thank and make sure the world knows about Amy Wolfe and her mission to help people remember that they are worthy. By creating signs, stickers, bracelets, and more she is sending a message to the world that we are enough. We are not our mistakes. She is helping people choose to live and not give up. She is an inspiration to us all.

Introduction

Who am I to write this book? Well, I'm a lot like you.

I've struggled with wanting to be perfect. Wanting to be understood. Wanting to be the best—but not the competitive best—just the person people turn to get it done. I wanted to be special. I wanted to be wanted.

I felt like I would be complete and have purpose if I could do enough. I worried all the time about doing enough for people, being too much of a burden, desiring too much, forgetting things, not getting good enough grades, not being grown up enough, not being able to hack it. What if I wasn't good enough?

I worked hard to make sure that there was something for everyone, that everyone was taken care of, that all needs were met. All needs but my own of course, because my needs would only be met by making sure everyone else's were.

I have been a chronic apologizer. I have been a black and white thinker. I worried all the time that I would fail and that it would be a catastrophe. I worried about what people would think of me and practiced how to respond to things before they would happen. I have always needed external rewards for what I do. Gold stars, A+'s, people commenting that they couldn't get along without me.

Does any of this sound familiar? I can go on—man, can I go on.

Over the last 40 years, I have learned some valuable lessons. Some from my own life and some from my career as a Licensed Psychologist. All of these lessons have changed the way that I think, act, and live my life.

I have compiled these lessons to help you live a life you haven't even imagined you could live. A life of fullness and enoughness. A life of worth. A life lived intentionally with less guilt, shame, and stress. A life of more hope, more success, and more love where you can be your best self.

Here are some things you might need to know about this book and me.

I have four core concepts:

1. Little "t" vs. big "T" truths.
2. Learning to make nonjudgmental, fully present, intentional choices.
3. Being aware of the words we use and how we use them.
4. You are enough—you have worth just by being you.

And, I am totally a nerd! I include some great movie quotes and nerdy references. Please let me know via social media when you find them; I want to nerd out with you.

Chapter 1: Little “t” vs. Big “T” Truth

> All the art of living lies in a fine mingling of letting go and holding on.
>
> *Henry Ellis*

My first core concept is “little ‘t’ vs. big ‘T’ truth.” I use it a lot in this book. In therapy, I often ask my clients “Is that a little ‘t’ or big ‘T’ truth?” I feel like using a capital letter indicates more significance than otherwise. We use them for names, places, things that are important. I use this strategy with little “t” vs. big “T” truths as an indicator that there are some beliefs that fall more into the category of opinions rather than the important actual *truths*. For instance, Mount Everest exists. Whether I believe it or not, this is a big “T” truth. Mount Everest is beautiful, is too far away to visit, or will last forever are little “t” truths. They are in fact momentary, changeable beliefs.

We write our own truths so much of the time. We tell ourselves, “I’m fat,” “I’m ugly,” “no one likes me.” Or “I am annoying,” “I’m rough around the edges,” “my family is crazy”—and on and on. We don’t actually weigh this with evidence, and much like the folks who thought the sun moved around us, we often will find out we are wrong. (Not about Pluto though... that’s messed up.) The reason we still call them truths (little “t”) is because we still believe them without the proof—and really, they end up being changeable when we have more information.

Sometimes we tell a story so many times that we are convinced it is true. Sometimes we take what someone in our family told us one time and hold that as truth. Sometimes we misinterpret a look, a feeling, or a touch and believe our interpretation to be true. When I was working with teen girls in residential treatment, I was called some terrible names. People who are hurting often lash out in anger, and boy, were those kids hurting. They also had learned some great self-defense mechanisms of finding people’s buttons or triggers to push people away. They recognized that I wanted to help them and I wanted to be liked. So, they called me names and told me they hated me. I was crushed. I went home crying and I asked my boss to move me to a different house because I was so hurt by what they said. I believed they were right. I believed the little "t" truth they were shouting at me. My boss asked a singular question, "Tara, are you a bitch?" Wide-eyed, shocked by this question, I realized the answer was "no." I was going home every night believing I was a bitch and a terrible person because a group of teenagers told me I was. But the big "T" truth was I am not a bitch. Once I realized the big "T" truth, those teens could call me names all they wanted but it didn't hold as much sway. Eventually, they stopped calling me "bitch" because it didn't work anymore.

Take a moment and think of something you believe to be true--about yourself, the relationships you are in, your family—whatever.

If I were to ask you how you could prove this was true, what could you come up with? Picture proof? Someone to corroborate the story, a scar or wound? Something you built? A videotape would be pretty good evidence, but would that prove it? Somethings may actually be true. You may be fat. But the deeper question to determine little "t" or big "T" truth is, does fat mean something more than the mass of your body in relation to the gravity of Earth? When people say they are fat they usually also mean ugly, gross, unattractive, not worth dating or being with. They don't just mean overweight. They mean *fat.* As a pejorative. So, let's dig into how we start finding the big "T" truth. Are you all those other words? Not necessarily. How would we even prove if you were ugly, gross, unattractive, and not worth it? Can we prove that to be true or is it an opinion? If it is an opinion, then we have a different conversation, don't we?

Big "T" truth is an important concept because there are so many things that we believe that *aren't* true. I could start with stories you have read on the internet, advertisements, fairy tales, Santa Claus—right? There are things that are easy to believe even if they aren't true

(Do this one thing and you will lose inches of belly fat!) But before you click on the bait, we need to do some digging to make sure the things we want to believe are true. And there are some things that are hard to believe even though they are true. (You have worth.)

Other significant influences on whether we believe something is true or not depends on where the information comes from. A blocked number calls and says you won a cruise. My first thought is, "Nope. Scam." If someone I love says, "You're despicable," my first thought is "What did I do? How can I fix this?" I don't question whether it is true or not. Because it came from someone I love. Ridiculous, right? You can see there is no proof, they only said some words. But we do this to ourselves all the time; we believe things without proof.

Sometimes when we struggle with our self-esteem, even someone we don't know can tell us something and we believe without questioning because we already think it about ourselves. It validates the opinion we have and becomes proof. If someone yells out their car window, "Hey, fatty!" I'm immediately self-conscious because I already have insecurities about that—so they have proven my insecurities right and thus. Bam! This must be *proof*. When actually it's just proof (little "p") because their opinion backs up what I already believe to be true, not because there is actual evidence.

When we speak of ourselves to others (or especially when we say things to ourselves) we often speak in definitive statements. Definitive statements can casually mask themselves as big "T" truths even when they are not. Take a look at some of these:

- I am lazy.
- I am terrible.
- I am worthless.
- I have no hope.
- This will never get better.
- This always happens to me.
- It is not worth trying.
- I always mess up.

- I will never finish.

You can see that we end up holding on to these as little "t" truths instead of looking for the big "T" truth. Holding on to a little "t" truth as if it were a big "T" truth is your own personal deception. And we do that a lot without realizing it! When we spend time deceiving ourselves—when we are not living intentionally—we are not living the way our best self would choose to live. Once we recognize this, we can start noticing that we are doing it. And once we notice that we are doing it, we can start to change it. So how do we find ways to make sure we are living in the big "T" truth intentionally?

The first way is to be aware when we make definitive statements and ask the question, "Are they little 't' or big 'T' truths?"

- I deserve to be alone vs. I feel alone.
- I am unwanted vs. I feel unwanted.
- I am unloved vs. I feel unloved.
- I am unattractive vs. I feel unattractive.
- There is no hope vs. it feels hopeless.

Adding an "I feel" or "it feels" in front of those sentences helps replace the mask of truth with an actual truth.

As you transform those definitive statements into what they really are (feelings, or little "t" truths) you then get to decide what to do about them.

Chapter 2: S.O.B.E.R. Skills

Today I will live in the moment. Unless the moment is unpleasant. Then today I will eat cookies.

Cookie Monster

I was teaching a class on Interventions at Pacific University and had a colleague come and teach about mindfulness. My understanding of mindfulness at the time was meditation. Yes, the exact meditation you are thinking of: sitting cross-legged and humming "ooomm." (And no wonder! One of my high school students told me "I hate mindfulness! I spent a semester doing that for P.E. and it was terrible. All my teacher did was have us lie on the floor in the gym with yoga mats and listen to beach sounds. And as nice as a nap is, what a waste of time!") Boy was I wrong. There is a lot more to mindfulness and meditation and incredible tools are available as well. One of them is represented by "S.O.B.E.R." This is a Mindfulness-Based Relapse prevention tool that is used to help people with addiction step back and make active choices about what they are doing.

Here is my "Sanderson-ized" version.

Take out a piece of paper. Yes, you could just read it. But it will be more solid in your mind if you just grab a piece of paper and follow the directions. Here's a pro tip: Writing things down helps decrease anxiety, helps increase understanding, and creates an opportunity to think rationally about things that may be causing you distress. The act of having to choose the words and put things in order helps decrease the stress on your brain as it tries to hold all those things in its active space. Next time you are stressed out or feeling overwhelmed, write down what is going on to get a little clarity.

Here's how I teach my clients this skill:

On the left side of your paper write the letters going down the page like this:

S

O

B

E

R

Then I want you to draw three dots.

•

•

•

Perfect! Gold Star!

Now to fill it in:

S – Stop

O – Observe

B – Breathe

E – Examine the options

R – Respond

Now for those bullet points:

- Non-Judgmentally
- Fully Present
- On Purpose

Let's add a few bits:

On the letter O, add in parentheses: (INSIDE and OUT)

On the letter B, add in parentheses: (5 Times)

On the Letter E, add in parentheses: (5 Options)

Phew!!! Now turn your paper 90 degrees counterclockwise (S.O.B.E.R. will be down at what is now the bottom of the page).

And write this word across the page in big bold letters along what is now the top (just straight on the page; we are not making an acronym with this):

INTENTIONAL

This is the goal of using this skill. This is the whole point of this chapter. To learn how to become intentional in our choices. The way that we do it is by practicing this S.O.B.E.R. skill.

Here's what it looks like all together

S - STOP

O - OBSERVE (Inside and out)

B - BREATHE (5x)

E - EXAMINE THE OPTIONS (5)

R - RESPOND (Pick one!)

- Non-Judgmentally
- Fully Present
- On Purpose

INTENTIONAL

Turn the page right side up. Now that you have your tool written down, let's walk through it.

Stop. This may seem obvious, but when do I stop? All the time. Any time you are making a decision. This can be a small decision—Do I add an extra scoop of chocolate chips to my mug cake? Or a big decision—Do I want to break up with my boyfriend, rent some kangaroos, or start school? When you begin a task, think about things, or just notice you are doing something, practice stopping that behavior, thought, or action. Next time you get in your car, stop before you reach for the car door, stop before you lift your foot to get into the car, stop before you put the key in the ignition. You get the point: Stop before you do everything and you will start to feel and see how many decisions you currently make unintentionally—or on autopilot! Now, I know many of you will say, "I get it. I don't need to practice it. I am going to skip this section and go to the good stuff." Well, my super friends, just like the Karate Kid, you have to start with the basics. (If you feel the need to go paint a fence or sand the deck right now, go for it. The book will be waiting for you when you get back.) When we start a new skill, we need to practice the basics in order to do it well. Practice stopping. Right now. Before you read the next sentence, stop.

Observe. This is the next step in the process of learning to make intentional choices. Observing is all about being fully present with what is happening both inside and outside of you. For me it is easier to do what is outside first: I assume that is because as an overachiever, perfectionistic, people-pleaser I am much more attuned to what is going on outside of me than what is going on inside of me. If I pay attention to what is outside of me, I can fix, find a solution, or proactively make things better for others. So, let's start with outside. As an example, when I work with clients, we have a discussion about using S.O.B.E.R. to decide if we are going to put our seatbelt on when we are driving home from the office. Many of my clients look at me and say, "Of course I am, it's the law." But the big "T" truth is, it is a choice whether or not to follow the law. I encourage clients (and you!) to think about this choice next time it comes up. Observe what is going on outside of you: Where am I going, who is around me, are there police around? Observe what is happening inside of you: Are you nervous, are you confident, are you hurried or futzing about?

That's how I explain it to my clients, and how I use observation in my own life, my relationship with food. I love food. I love salt, I love sweet, I love bread, I love butter, I love meat. I love all sorts of things. (I am also a super picky eater, a-butter-has-to-be-completely-melted-on-the-bread-before-I-will-eat-it kind of picky). When I'm on autopilot I could eat a whole cake, a whole jar of peanut butter, a whole bag of mini chocolate chips, or huge amounts of McDonald's French fries—all without stopping, without thinking. And I have. I have absolutely sat in my kitchen in secret and silence eating handfuls of mini chocolate chips while cooking, not at all thinking about what I am doing. Just scoop in, scoop in.

As I practice living intentionally, I notice some things. First, I have to give myself some grace. It can take me ten minutes to stop sometimes. Ten minutes is a long time in the land of mini chocolate chips! Once I choose to stop, I start observing: What is going on outside me? (Am I cooking, am I waiting for something, is this the only sweet thing in the house?) What is going on inside of me? (Am I anxious, do I feel deprived, am I hungry, am I upset, am I happy?) As I ask questions and find answers, I get the information to make better choices. But don't rush to that just yet! We have more steps to go and they are important. This part of the process is all about exploring. Exploring with no agenda. Exploring with just your senses, brain, and heart. It is vital that you approach this step with the eyes of someone who is just watching what is happening without judgment. We will save ourselves a lot of self-loathing and judgment here if we are able to just be patient and watch, record, and observe.

Breathe. In my experience, this is the one step everyone wants to skip. I can't tell you how many times I have heard in therapy, "Deep breathing doesn't work for me. I would rather do something else." Now if it does work for you, good on you! Keep doing it! If you don't think it works for you, try again! In fact, try multiple kinds of breathing each time you do S.O.B.E.R. Try Dragon Breathing or Square Breathing (see appendix for some great examples of breathing exercises). Taking these deep breaths has two goals. First, to take some time to step away from the decision action or behavior and reset. Space between action, behavior, and intentional choice are important. What is one of the first things we try to teach children? Think first before you act. My dad used the adage: "measure twice, cut once" when we worked on building things in the garage. Same thing! Take your time. Second, to continue to practice doing something intentionally. Taking those five breaths with focus and purpose will help you practice being focused and in the moment. Right now—stop and take five deep breaths. If you have a cool app on your phone or watch to breathe along with, use that. Or if you enjoy being more low-tech, just count out the five breaths as you take them.

Examine the Options. Now you can put your problem-solving skills to work. I want you to think of five options. Two of them should be extreme options. Three should be more moderate or middle ground. Here are examples of five options that I use with teens when they are mad at their parents/teachers:

1. You could run away to the circus (yes, that is still totally a possibility).
2. You could punch them in the face.
3. You could walk to your room or to a quiet space.
4. You could tell them you are upset.
5. You could ask for space to calm down.

These are actual options.

Next, I usually follow up with, "And if you choose option 1 or option 2, you will need to do it using the three bullet points: non-judgmentally, fully present, and on purpose." The choice most kids laugh at is punching the adult in the face. I tell them, "Well if you are going to do that, you will need to be able to form your fist just right, really put your whole body into that punch, and be 100% sure and focused on doing it. And not feel bad about it." Most kids look at me and say, "I could never do that!" (Rest assured; I don't use this example with anyone in the conduct disorder spectrum!) I tell them, "You could make that choice, but it doesn't sound like you want to make that choice." Once we eliminate the options we don't want to do, we examine the other options.

Back to my mini chocolate chips. Once I have stopped and observed and breathed, I take a look at my options. I could:

1. Keep eating until the bag is gone.
2. Put the bag away.
3. Have one more handful and then put the bag away.
4. Tell my husband what I am doing.
5. Leave the bag on the counter for a few minutes to put a little space between us.

I wonder if you can guess the extremes? (With 1 and 4, guilt and shame in my eating game get me every time! Truth is I know my husband already knows what I am doing and he is a supportive guy who will help when I am ready.)

Respond. The next section is all about making a choice. Picking an option. Simple. Just pick. Any of them are fine. Any of them will be okay. None of them will be permanently detrimental to the world (except murder; don't murder people!). This is an area where we get tripped up. Is there a better choice, is there a wrong choice? They are all just choices. All choices can be reversed (except murder; see above). I will also say that there are some other choices that are close to the black and white edges that should be looked at through the lens of ethics and morals before you make them. But for the purposes of this book and all you compliant overachievers out there, they are likely not the choices we are talking about. In addition, remember the three bullet points we made earlier. Your choice will be dependent on weighing those three bullet points. Know that you will be analyzing your choice a bit further and making your decisions with some support! (Even now I want to take my time with this concept because if you are like me at all you cringed at the idea that there are no wrong choices. "Of course there are wrong choices!" we might say. Take a deep breath! There are choices in all shades of grey. Most of them will not be in the black or white zone; there really aren't very many that are truly right or wrong).

Once you have picked an option and are ready to move forward, start with the "weighing test." Here are the 3 bullet points from S.O.B.E.R.:

- Non-Judgmentally
- Fully Present
- On Purpose

The weighing test goes like this:

- Can I pick this option and not judge myself poorly for this decision?
- Can I pick this option and do it being fully present?
- Can I pick this option and do it on purpose?

If the answer is "no" to any of these questions, go back to the responses and pick a different option. Then do the weighing test again.

If the answer is yes, great! Go forth with your decision!

Back to my chocolate chip example: If I say, "Yes! I can eat this whole bag with reckless abandon and do it with no judgment, fully present. and on purpose," I can sit down on the couch with my chocolate chips and go for it. If I can get through the bag making that choice with no guilt, judgment, or blame—awesome! I made an intentional choice. If I can't, because I notice I am starting to say, "Ugh, what am I doing?" Or, "I should stop, I feel gross," or I notice I am not enjoying it or being fully present (thinking and liking every bite verses just shoveling them in)—then I start over at the top and use S.O.B.E.R. again.

Stop, Observe, Breathe, Examine the Options, Respond. I go through this process over and over until I am making an intentional choice. A choice I can make non-judgmentally, fully present, and on purpose.

I have talked about making decisions intentionally, but why is it important to make decisions intentionally? Well, how many times can you remember sitting in your space (car, home, boat, own head) ruminating over your choices? We say things like, "I should have done it this way." Or, "I shouldn't have said that." Sometimes we have said or done things without purpose, or spoken so quickly without thinking that we then regret what we said. As anxious folks, we regret and relive our choices because we weren't being intentional. I have two really strong memories about saying the wrong things that still plague me.

1. For my birthday when I was younger (maybe 13) a friend of mine gave me some earrings. They were gold hoops. I remember opening the box and saying, "I don't like gold." Now, I was raised to say thank you and to write thank you cards and to be kind. But in that unintentional moment, I spoke four words that hurt my friendship and I still carry those words around. (I don't struggle with those four words every day, but I would love to find that friend now and apologize!) I was not fully present in the moment. I wasn't being purposeful about my words. And as a result, I struggle with judging myself about that choice. In other words, I wasn't being intentional.

2. I was at work one day and a coworker was showing off her new car. I remember standing in the doorway of the home, looking out at her car in the driveway and saying out loud, "I would never drive one of those." Ugh! Didn't I learn from the gold earrings (judgment)?

Some of my clients have asked me, "Isn't reframing just lying?" Nope. Reframing is putting information into a new perspective. When we put information into a new perspective, hopefully, we use our S.O.B.E.R. skills and analyze the big picture to decide how we want to move forward with intent. I never encourage you to lie to people. Lying might look like me saying, "Oh thanks! These are my favorite!" for some gold earrings. Instead, using some intentional word choice I could say, "These are so beautiful," or, "I am so thankful you thought of me." In the instance of the car, lying might look like "Wow! Your car is so awesome" when I don't believe that. Instead, I could say "What do you like most about this car?" Or "You seem to really love this car! Good for you." I do want to be intentional, and be fully present, and with purpose relate to and connect with the person. All these things that fit my values and my need to connect with people. That is me living intentionally.

Chapter 3: I Want A Syllabus For This Part of My Life

> We must be willing to get rid of the life we've planned so as to have the life that is waiting for us.
>
> *Joseph Campbell*

I started pondering this book when I was finishing up grad school and thought, "Oh Crap!" For 20-odd years, someone has given me a piece of paper every September (or so) and told me what my life was going to be like over the next nine months. Then I got a couple months' break and did it all over again. I felt great relief that first day of school when handed that syllabus. I knew for sure what was expected of me. Where I was supposed to be, what I was going to learn, what the rules were. I knew where I was going to sit and how to be perfect. Phew! All my fears laid to rest. Now all I had to do was do it. Follow directions. Be in the right place at the right time. Easy peasy.

Fast forward. They handed me a cap and gown. A diploma and said, "Great job! You did it. Have a nice life."

What?!!?!?! Where is my next syllabus? What do I do next? I mean yes—there are the "in general" societal rules: you get a job, find a partner, settle down, have a family, buy a house, work work work all the time, save for retirement, retire, watch your kids and grandkids grow, die.

But those rules are too general. How do you pick a job, pick a partner, pick a house? Do you get to choose to have a family? Settle down? Retire? What if you do something wrong? Anxiety rises.

A syllabus would sure help. I know many people who said, "Well, I'll just be a student forever." (Ahem. My husband clears his throat, "You said that," he says. "Yeah, well, I know other people too!" I respond sheepishly). I went on after my doctorate to get my MBA in non-profit management so I could run the company I was working for at the time and to be able to understand the finance, marketing, and facilitation of a business. After that, I thought, "I really want to understand the concepts behind social work." So I started looking into a program for an MSW. I thought a double doctorate sounded cool. What if I went back and got my doctorate in business administration? That would be awesome. But honestly, I was just looking for something to structure my life. I wanted another syllabus. Something to help me play by the rules and follow the clear directions. Something to give me lines to color inside of.

Not having lines means I can mess up. I can veer off course. I am in charge now, and what if I mess up? What if there is no coming back from where I end up? Anxiety rises.

But the big "T" truth is this: There is nothing you can't come back from (outside of murder; don't murder people). You will make choices and can make new ones. You are very rarely stuck forever with the decisions you have made. You can create your own structure by way of your beliefs, values, efforts, and energies. You don't need someone directing your life, giving you instructions, or putting lines out for you to follow. You are capable of making your own intentional decisions, changing your mind, and making new decisions as needed.

Setting an agenda for the day, creating my own structure, and navigating my own path are ways I have found success. I sit each morning with my planner, my phone, and my honey lemon water and create an agenda for the day. I write down my intentions (drinking water, exercising, calling my grandmother) and my to-do's (dishes, sweeping, writing my notes, doing my writing for this here book, and other things like checking the mail or appointments). I reflect on yesterday's commitments and accomplishments and look ahead at the rest of my week and put together a plan to make it all happen. When I do this, I am setting a syllabus for myself. Sometimes my schedule includes self-care items like getting a massage. Sometimes things like unpacking *everything* from my move, which can totally be self-care. Sometimes it is just boring life stuff like cleaning the shower.

The thing about them is *all* those things are things I chose to do. Things that I can give myself a gold star on, things that will set me up for success and allow me to live my values and feel good about them. None of them will get a gold star from the universe. As we know there aren't actually gold stars from the universe.[1] You have to give them to yourself.[2]

1 Although if you find out how to get a gold star from the universe – please let me know. I *need* that gold star.

2 Or me. You can give me gold stars any time you want!

Chapter 4: What do you mean I am a grown up?

There will be moments when you have to be a grown-up. Those moments are tricks. Don't fall for them.

Jenny Lawson

That moment when there is a situation that needs wisdom and you are looking for an adult, but you realize that you are an adult. So you look around for an older adult, an adultier adult. Someone better at adulting than you.

Unknown

What do you mean I am a grown up? This feels like the question of the season. Adulting, growing up, being responsible. How many times have you seen "I can't adult today" on a poster or on a coffee cup? Every time I see those words, I recognize that I am not alone on this journey to become an adult. It's everywhere, and honestly, I get it. When I graduated college and got my first "real" job at the Family Care Network doing in-home counseling for teens, then I knew what being a grown-up was. Right?

Then I went to grad school out of state and signed a rental agreement on a place. I took out student loans in my own name. I had to buy real groceries and supplies for life. And then I was really a grown-up.

Then I met my husband and bought a house. Dealing with all the weird stuff that comes with home ownership, I must be a grown-up now.

Then I refinanced my home, dealt with homeowner's insurance claims, and started an IRA. Total grown up, right?

Over the course of the years, I have bought and sold cars, houses, and started my own business. I have filed my taxes, had an accountant, made good choices and hard choices. I have been on the very edge of my financial accounts, learned to budget, and tracked my food choices. I have had a primary care physician, purchased my own insurance, and made some tough decisions regarding my health. This means I'm finally a grown-up right?

But what does it even mean to be a grown-up?

If, as you are reading this book, you are hoping for someone to just give you a plan to make it all work, there are plenty of "how-to" self-help books out there. But here's the trick. The only plan or syllabus that will work for you is the one *you* make. The one you are intentionally living. The path you are on. The choices that you make. That's it. There can be only one. You can read all the books, and from them, you can gather what works for you. You can learn the tricks and tips that best fit you, and you will make the decisions that best fit your situation. Well, here's to growing up.

Being a grown-up is all about problem solving, making choices, and managing expectations. That's it. Hook, line, and sinker.

Problem-solving. When I was training new employees to help teach problem-solving to teens, I would explain it this way: Everything is a learning opportunity. And if there isn't an obvious learning opportunity, make one. For instance, I often take the kids to the mall. During the mall trip we work on social skills, we work on budgeting and planning, we work on politeness. These are obvious learning opportunities. Then we walk out to the car to go home. What can you learn from walking out to the car? Nothing really, until I tell them I have locked my keys in the car. Then we have a problem-solving activity to work on. We brainstorm at least ten ways to get home. Usually, one of the kids grabs a rock and says, "I can get them out." And we talk about the pros and cons of that decision. It would cost $300 to fix the window. It would be the fastest way, but there would be glass everywhere that we would have to clean up before we could go home. Lots of cons—not a lot of pros. We also talk about when that might be appropriate: If I was being chased by a serial killer or zombie? Worth it. We talk about calling a tow truck (approximate cost $75; probably a half hour to an hour until it arrives). But the truck could get there and the tech could fix it fast and we could get on our way. A good number of pros; the only cons are money and time. When would that be appropriate? When you don't have anywhere else to be, or when you have a lot of money. We talk about calling a friend with a key. Costs zero, but our wait would be more than an hour. When would that be appropriate? When would it not? What are ways you can remember to keep your keys with you instead of locking them in the car? What are some pros of that? What are some cons?

Problem-solving comes down to narrowing the choices between ideas to the one for which you are willing to pay the cost (literal and figurative). Problem-solving flexibility comes from building layers of options and engaging creative thinking to help support your ideas and facilitate growth.

Why is this important? Well, as a grown-up, there are a lot of things you will need to be able to do. A lot of questions you will need to have answered. Why is my fridge making that sound? When do I need to call an electrician instead of trying to do it myself? When is it time to get a new job? Should I pay for this with credit or cash? There are no right or wrong answers. Just answers that will get you to your goals, answers that will take you further from them, or answers that will leave you sitting right where you are now.

This is why S.O.B.E.R. is such an important tool. Using this tool, you have to come up with multiple solutions to the same situation. And because of that, you are working on expanding your problem-solving skill set. The more you grow that skill set, the easier adulting is going to be for you.

When I choose to go out to eat, I have to process this based on many levels and goals. Let's look at four of the goals I have in my life right now: losing weight, enjoying life, spending time with friends, and saving money. All of these are import and valuable to me. When I am aware of my goals and am using S.O.B.E.R. skills, I can be intentional about how I make that choice. When I am examining the options, I can come up with a variety of choices to decide what fits my goals and values at this time. What is the price I am willing to pay at this time for this activity? I can choose to do things anyway I want. It's up to me. None of these decisions is right or wrong, each is just a choice, and each choice has a cost and a benefit that I will need to look at in order to make the decision non-judgmentally, fully present, and on purpose.

Now that we understand problem-solving and how beneficial it is to being a grown-up, let's move on to making choices.

Making choices. Sometimes my clients are shocked when I tell them they have a choice in everything. We feel like we don't. We feel like there are some musts, and some must nots. We feel like there are things we get to choose, but not everything! But the big "T" truth is they are all choices. You can choose whether to get out of bed today, whether to drive or walk to work, or whether to go at all. You have a choice in whether to be nice to people or to be a jerk. You have a choice in everything.

Why is it important to remember we have choices all the time? Well, because we are often only limited by our own understanding and our own thoughts. When we put a box around the "must-dos" we take away our choice and this can limit our ability to live intentionally. Same goes with "must-not-dos." When we take away the choice to try something, we remove the possibility of living intentionally.

We can minimize that limited thinking by using our S.O.B.E.R. skills and making intentional decisions about everything. Imagine if you were able to wake up in the morning and do everything that would make your day amazing. What do you think would happen? You'd probably have an amazing day! Wouldn't that be great? Why wouldn't we choose that? We often don't choose it because we are on autopilot and don't make intentional choices. That's why.

When I am stressed, I often skip the steps that would make my day amazing. I press snooze on my alarm. I skip my workout and don't take time to prioritize my day – thinking I am giving myself some self-care and more time. As I move through my morning I am sluggish and wish I had more time. I find myself not packing my lunch, then feeling like my only option is to eat out during the day, which ultimately leads me away from my goals and leaves me feeling terrible. If I rewind my day and make intentional choices at each stop along the way... would I make the choice to feel terrible? Or would I choose to do the things that make me feel my best? When I run on autopilot (the easiest route) I often find that it leads not to feeling amazing... but to wishing I had made intentional choices.

Making choices using S.O.B.E.R. skills creates an avenue for intentional living. And being an intentional living adult is the epitome of being an awesome adult.

Managing expectations. There are two core elements to managing expectations as an adult. First, set realistic, appropriate, manageable expectations. Second, be able to be flexible when expectations aren't met.

My husband teaches classes to help folks get back into the job market. During those classes, he touches on the subject of expectations verses reality. That conversation has led me to some interesting conversations with my clients—and with myself. As an overachiever, I believe I need to do everything well. Fast, well, cheap, best—everything. I graduated from college in three years instead of four because I pushed myself to do so. I thought it would give me an edge for what comes next. (At the time I thought I was just going to move back to my hometown, meet a guy, and be a grown-up!) And maybe graduating early did give me an edge, but it didn't turn out as expected. Does it ever? Think of how many times you have gone down the rabbit trail of "what ifs" and found yourself at the end with all the answers to all the "what ifs" and found that that time spent was useful and prepared you for what was coming next? Rarely, if ever. But that doesn't mean we don't try, right? We are actively trying to prepare ourselves in our anxious, overcompensating brains! If we can prepare for it all, we won't have to sit with that icky feeling of not knowing what is going to happen. But even if we try to find all the right answers, our expectations don't usually fit the reality. Whether it is something we didn't predict or it is something that we couldn't anticipate, or maybe we just weren't being honest with ourselves.

There are two parts to this:

1. I set the expectation too high ("I am going to lose 150 pounds this year") or,
2. I expect (believe/hope) things will turn out the way that I want—not the way they might (the "it's not fair" scenario).

That is a sucky thing to figure out: that our expectations—that people will do what I want them do, will be kind, will follow through with things, will not leave—is not always reality. People can be jerks sometimes; they do leave; things do end.

One of the lessons I think we learn the hard way is that just because we believe something is right, doesn't mean others will think the same. You are coming from your best intentions—and they are coming from theirs.

When we start to confront these expectations, we find we fall into several camps:

- The "it's-not-fair" camp
- The "of-course-you-are-right" camp

- The "guess-this-is-the-way-it-goes" camp
- The "universe-is-out-to-get-me" camp
- The "maybe-next-time" camp

These camps keep us in our angst against the reality that people all make their choices. We make ours when we set our expectations at an unattainable level. We know that this leads to disappointment and frustration. We see the impact of others' choices when we experience the disappointment that they didn't meet our need.

None of these, of course, is a part of the acceptance, stand-up-for-yourself, or ask-for-what-you-need camps; those are real too! And I think as we start to grow through the feelings of understanding that our expectations may not live up to reality, we can start to integrate all these camps and find some peace with life as it is—not how we want it to be or wish it was or long for it to be again.

So how do we set manageable expectations? We take a step back. We take a look at the reality; we remove the lens that tells us anything is possible and we settle in with the truth. For example, I want to lose some weight. My goal is to lose 100 pounds. Can I lose 100 pounds in a year? Yes, that is technically possible—but is it possible for me? That will depend on lots of things! Am I willing to commit to giving up certain things this year to make that happen? Am I willing to add in more working out to make that happen? Am I willing to commit financially to that goal? If not, then losing 100 pounds this year is not manageable. Taking a step back and analyzing what I am willing to do for the goal I am setting allows me to adjust my expectations to something reasonable.

The next element of managing expectations is being able to be flexible when expectations aren't met. This is a tough one for me. I was introduced to this statement the other day:

Inflexible rules = unhappy life

As a rule-oriented person, I love rules and the structure they offer. I find great pleasure in knowing a rule and following it.

But having inflexible rules can create more chaos than having flexibility in our thinking. Inflexible rules are rules we create to give meaning, pursue justice, or create a rhythm to our lives. They are also the things that can hold us back from being happy.

Let's look at some inflexible rules.

When going to a Christmas party at a friend's house I know exactly who is going to be there. Then I get a text as we are parking in the parking lot: "Oh, I invited so-and-so and so-and-so now there are 15 people at the party." (Okay, so it really was just three new people added, but it felt like 15 at this point!) Boom. My heart sinks. I don't even want to go to the party now. In fact, I am so bummed that the plans changed my face shows it (and I can most of the time have a pretty good poker face, except for when my husband is watching; he always seems to know). And when my face shows it my husband knows he has to help me make the transition from my previous expectation to the new truth. It will be different than I expected.

And maybe that is the thing about inflexible rules—inflexible rules mean we have specific expectations. And when those expectations aren't met, we are unhappy, uncomfortable, and not okay.

Inflexibility can then trigger issues with selfishness, unworthy-ness, frustration with ourselves—and our partners may even get triggered by this.

So we have to start allowing things to be different than we anticipated. We have to adjust our expectations. We have to start removing the rigidity and begin to allow things to be more flexible.

Flexibility is key when we want to be happy—assuming that is your goal! This book is all about giving you some structure to set your life up so that you can be happy. You can have that, but the structure is not pure syllabus style—you can't get an "A" in life. You get to learn all sorts of lessons, supports and designs on life's journey, and how you put it together will determine your level of happiness. Like I have said: I need a morning routine to set me on a good path during the day. But if my routine is interrupted, I need to use my flexibility skills to help me make a new plan and do something different. Being flexible allows me to be successful. Rigidity or inflexible rules don't give me that in the same way.

When we hope that rules will give us the structure we need and that if we follow the rules, we will get an "A," we are headed in the wrong direction. The universe doesn't give out A's or gold stars. Those come from you.

Inflexible rules = an unhappy life. And if you were going to choose—intentionally—would you choose an unhappy life? We are convinced the rules give us the option for that good feeling when we have met them because following the rules has always given us that good feeling—but not this time. (Well, kind of this time; you can feel good following the rules. The rules aren't bad.) The thing that makes it harder is the inflexibility. It is one thing to follow the rules and feel good about it. It is another thing to be so inflexible about change that the rules make you feel like crap. Or they make you blow off a Christmas party because it doesn't meet the expectation you set for yourself.

Living in the here and now and being intentional about choices gives us the ability to accept the things that are, ask for what we need, tolerate that life is not fair. The universe can dole out some whoppers, but know at the end of the day—we can handle it. We are that good. You are that good. You have survived every single day up to this point—you can survive this day too.

Chapter 5: Fear of failing in public

Failure is a bruise, not a tattoo.

Jon Sinclair

I can't remember a time in grade school, junior high, or high school that I ever raised my hand in class unless I was required to in order to get a grade. I remember the feeling of knowing the answer but being way too scared that maybe I was wrong and I shouldn't risk it. I remember talking with my teachers and asking if I could just give them the answers before or after class. I remember struggling with my breathing and heart rate any time a teacher called on me in class.[3]

You might have lived in fear of failing in front of others your whole life. You might know exactly where it came from; you might only know you have always felt this way. Either way, failing is uncomfortable. Failing is a big word. And most of the time failing is a little "t" truth. We aren't actually failing; we just aren't doing something the way we expected it to be done. We are actually worried about what other people will think.

Wow. What a feeling this brings up. Embarrassment, shame, frustration, worry about people realizing I am not perfect, the frustration

---

3 And then of course there was track and field in junior high. We were supposed to run hurdles. I was afraid of tripping over the hurdle and falling flat on my face. It wasn't afraid I'd hurt myself; I was afraid I'd fall in front of everyone. When it was my turn to run the course, I created an outside lane—one that didn't have hurdles in it. I leaped over the imaginary hurdles and hoped to get a grade for that. I was able to clear the imaginary hurdles but my teacher didn't think it was the same, so I failed that part of my track and field class. My teacher let us fail one part of the class without it affecting our grade. She said not everyone is good at everything, but everyone needs to try, so my final grade was okay. I could minor fail the activity and still pass the class. And I didn't end up on my face.

and belief that now that everyone knows they can't un-see it. Feeling like people are going to feel bad for me or feel sorry for me. Ugh! I feel all that deeply in my chest as I write this.

I know you know that feeling. You are likely cringing as you read this and thinking, "Oh no!"

How many of you have ever watched a movie where the actor does something—falls in front of people or messes up in some way and everyone is watching—and you have that same gross feeling where you are embarrassed for them. Even though it is only a movie? I have. All the time.

But the hardest moment of my educational career was when I was put on academic probation in graduate school. I had been on academic probation my first year in college because my ACT test score indicated I put my name on the paper. (I am not sure they actually give you points for that, but you know what I mean.) I had a lot of trouble with standardized tests and that one, I am confident, I napped through. I rushed through questions and napped between sections. I got the score I deserved for the effort I put in. I believed a little "t" truth: "I'm not good at standardized tests." So I didn't put effort into them. When they put me on probation I understood why and knew that my classwork would make it clear that I was kind of a badass when it came to school and they would lift the probation in no time. (At the time I was crushed, but I remember the story now with fondness! And they did lift it after the first semester because I rocked all A's and worked full time; they figured I was alright. I also then went on to do my entire BA degree in three years instead of four while working full time. Right? Rockstar. Give me my gold stars, please!)

But grad school was different. In grad school I got good grades, turned in all my assignments, worked full time—and they said it wasn't good enough. *What*? Not good enough at school? I was awesome at school! How could it not be good enough? My advisors told me the problem: I wasn't speaking up in class. Ugh. I feel heaviness in my chest as I write. They said, "Tara, you need to speak in class. You need to be a part of the conversation. Your opinion is important and we need to see you engaging in the material." Ugh.

So they introduced the "two cents." One of my advisors gave me two pennies, symbolizing giving my "two cents" in class. He asked that I take them to every class and set them in front of me to remind me to speak up at least two times in every class. Ugh. Not only was I embarrassed to speak in class for fear of being wrong—let alone fear of being found out to be an imposter who didn't belong in graduate school, let alone in a doctoral program—but now I had to physically have two cents in front of me every day. One positive from this was I received a clear outline of the expected behavior. And I am good at compliance. I can follow directions well. You tell me to speak two times in every class, and I can come off the naughty list—done. Two cents. Every class. Every time. Done. It is just meeting an expectation and I am good at doing that.

Choosing to do it for myself was the next task. I stayed on academic probation for quite a bit of my educational career in grad school, mostly because I didn't believe that I was actually worth hearing. I spent so much of my time worried about failing in the eyes of my peers, my teachers, and myself that I didn't embrace the actual abilities I did have. Intense thoughts went through my head daily, thoughts that my peers would think I was dumb. My professors would think I shouldn't be in grad school. Every time I spoke in class I thought, "This could be my last chance to be here. What if I say something dumb?" or "What if I am wrong? What if they all find out I am a fake?" Those thoughts rolled like a freight train through my mind each class period. Did you find all the little "t" truths I was believing? I bet if you really look you could find at least 5 in this paragraph. (While you are at it, keep an eye out for Waldo, I'm pretty sure he is hidden in here somewhere too.)

I can say now that I know that I am smart. I know that I have a lot to share with others and that I am worth listening to. But it took a long time for me to realize that. I carried that little "t" truth that it would be easier for others to have low expectations of me. The alternative was that they have high expectations and I might not meet those some of the time, which would fuel the feeling that I was a failure. Easier is totally the wrong word—it was less *uncomfortable* for me if others had low expectations for me. It seems less uncomfortable to sit back and not tell people my big, bad, crazy, lovely dreams, because what if they don't come true? What if I am wrong? What if I fail?

My husband is so interesting with his family. (Interesting to me because I am not like this with mine, or with my friends, or with him—see a theme here?) When he goes home and chats with his family, he shares with them not only the things he has done, but things he is thinking about doing. He processes with them why he is thinking that way and asks what they think about it. He is open to suggestions and is able to hear them when they say, "Oh! Don't do that; here's a better way." Now, my husband does a lot of research on things that he invests in most of the time. And sometimes he's impulsive. (Okay. So sometimes we are both impulsive.) But the point is he usually works hard at making sure he has thought through all the angles and is making a good decision. It's awesome. I feel so safe and so supported. And it is amazing because he doesn't fear his family's response. He doesn't seem to fear anyone's response; he is confident in his thought process and open to having someone disagree.

Not me. I didn't really even tell my husband I wanted to write a book until about ten years into our marriage. When I did tell him, he said, "That sounds amazing. How can I help?" After we talked about it for a while he said, "You know, if you tell me you want to do something, I will totally help you get there." And that is Big "T" True. I don't have to worry about failing with him. And yet, I do worry about it. What if he finds out that I am not exactly what he was looking for? What if I am not actually smart, or I am not going to be able to make this book happen? That fear. That embarrassment. That worry.

Chapter 5: Fear of failing in public

At the end of this book, I am going to include a list of words. Words mean something and are important, but this is a list of words to which we often attach value or judgment, and we need to read them as neutral. These words are just words, words that indicate something is happening—not good or bad or otherwise. One of the words on this list is *failure.*

Failure = a lesson to be learned, not a tragic falling apart of your world. Not a place you can't come back from. Not a terrible thing. *Failure* doesn't have any good or bad connotation. It just is something to learn from. How many failures did the inventor of the lightbulb face before it worked? What about vaccines? Or automatic dishwashers? How many times did you have to fall down while you were learning to walk? Those were technically failures too. They led to you walking, running, and dancing!

I put *failure* on that list so we can reframe its definition and learn to ask the question, "What have I learned from this?" We can become more comfortable with failure if we can tap into our curious side. The side of us that wants to understand and know things. Because if we understand and know things, we can excel at them. (See what I did there?) We can't be afraid of doing things and failing if we want to eventually master them. (Well, we can be afraid and we are a lot of the time. But the hope is that we are growing and instead of needing to always have an "A" in everything with very little effort or trial, we get comfortable learning how to do things.) We learn from failures and accept our B/C/D/F status at things we have yet to master in life.

Was that painful to hear? I bet some of you were immediately thinking, "Excuse me? You want me to be okay with failing?" Some of you saw the letters B/C/D/F and started hyperventilating and wanted to quit reading. You were hoping I wasn't serious. But I was. One of the Big "T" truths is you are not an "A" student in everything. There I said it. And it is okay.

I bet some of you are contemplating skipping the rest of this chapter right now because you don't want to get an "F." You don't want to be comfortable with a "B."

But here's the thing: You are not an 'A" all around.

Mic. Drop.

You are amazing, wonderful, creative, intelligent, and awesome. But you are not perfect. You are not a 4.0 at life. You can't just do things perfectly right the first time and get your good grades to prove that you are okay. Grades and perfect don't have anything to do with you being okay.

Chapter 6: Fear of being rejected

> Do Something uncomfortable today. By stepping out of your box, you don't have to settle for what you are—you get to create who you want to become."
>
> *Howard Wolstein*

In my experience as a psychologist, I often hear that people fear rejection. Even in my personal life, I recognize the struggles that we humans have wanting to be wanted and fearing being rejected. Lots of people fear being rejected. It is scary to think that someone you like could decide they don't like you. It might be worse if you have already had some big rejections in your life.

Big "T" truth is we all get rejected at one time or another.

Not everyone is going to like us.
Not everyone is going to want to be with us and hang out with us.
We are not going to get an "A" in this part of our life.

Are you still there? Good. I just laid down some hard truths. These hurt a bit. And yet, these are truths nonetheless. It is so important to understand these truths, even though it hurts.

Being rejected is something we learn from, something we are supposed to feel and understand, and something we can find ways to navigate on a regular basis.

Fear of rejection often comes from the core belief that I am not worth being around. When we look at it this way, we recognize that it isn't so much about the other person rejecting us. It is more about the confirmation of our little "t" truth that I'm not worth being around. And if we dig deeper and funnel that down, we might also find these little "t" truths: "I am not worthy," "I am not important," "I don't deserve love."

Ouch. Those words hurt. I hear those words every day when my clients speak. When they call themselves stupid, worthless, dumb, childish, selfish, horrible. What they are really saying is "I don't have value on my own. I don't bring anything to the table. I am not worthy. I don't deserve love."

When we put ourselves out there (which is hard to do) and someone says "no thanks" (or even worse, rudely rejects us or ignores us), this seems to validate our core belief that we are not lovable. That we are not important or valuable. That we are not enough.

Are these big "T" truths?

And really, whose opinion of you defines who you are? Is it a boyfriend, parent, best friend, stranger at the bar or coffee shop? Is it the guy who is scanning your groceries? Is it the woman on the phone from the cable company? Should they impact the big "T" truth of who you are and that you matter? These people have opinions about who you are.

Everyone has opinions. We have them about everything—from what goes on a pizza to how people should act at a funeral. A great movie from Pixar called *Inside Out* portrays how we learn to deal with our emotions. At one point a character knocks over two boxes. One box says "Facts" and the other says "Opinions." And she says "Oh, no! These facts and opinions look so alike—I'll never be able to get them back where they were." Her friend says, "Don't worry. It happens all the time," and he just scoops some up and puts them back in whatever box is nearby.

Yep. That is how we treat facts and opinions sometimes. Over the past year this has come up consistently with clients. We have had to work through the difference between opinions and facts. But *opinions aren't truth*. They are your way of seeing the world. They are your understanding of the world and your current belief. And opinions change. You may have been staunchly against something as a young child and now you are okay with it. You may have been fully in support of something a few years ago and are now totally against it. Your opinion changes.

Truth doesn't change. Your understanding of truth might change. Our interpretation of the information surrounding truth might change, but the truth doesn't change.

The *truth* is—you are worthy of love. You do have worth and value just as you are. You are enough.

There are no caveats or "only ifs" or "when I..." You just are enough. When you are able to believe that—when you can hold this knowledge deep in that sacred space where truth lives in your soul—things like being rejected aren't so scary. It doesn't matter if people don't like you. You are already okay as you are. If the person you have given ten years of your life to decides to leave, it will hurt like crazy. But you are worthy of love. You do have worth and value and you are enough. With or without that person. You have *worth.*

Chapter 7: Imposter syndrome

> You will never speak to anyone more than you speak to yourself in your head, be kind to yourself.
>
> *Unknown*

In psychology we learn that we will often feel like we are imposters doing the job we have chosen. It feels like this in other industries too. Before I learned the term *imposter syndrome*, I felt it in my other jobs. I was sitting at a desk at Karla Kool Realty having taken over the job of a secretary from a woman in her 30s who was off to have a baby. At the ripe age of 17, I thought "Oh, no! What is going to happen when they realize I don't have a clue what I am doing?" Imposter syndrome.

Moms feel it when they look at their child and think, "Crap! I am just making this up as I go along!"

Husbands feel it (mine does, he actually says "I am just making this up as I go along" *all the time*).

Children feel it when they are learning new concepts and hoping that they get it right.

Employees, employers, writers, teachers, trainers, chiropractors, doctors—all feel imposter syndrome. When you are sensitive to failure, when you have struggles with your self-esteem, when you wish that perfection really was an option, when you have high expectations—you feel this. Imposter syndrome. These all sound a lot like little "t" truths, don't they?

I remember when I got my bachelor's degree—walking with that robe and my cords from Psi Chi—I thought, "Shouldn't I know more about all this psychology stuff by now? I mean I have a BA in it! I should go get my master's and doctorate—then I'll really know my stuff." I walked two more times with robes and got pieces of paper saying I know my business when it comes to psychology. And still I felt like I don't know everything! Shouldn't I know everything if I am going to have a *doctorate* in this? All of those "shoulds" highlight my little "t" truth that college (or grad school, or a doctorate) will teach me everything.

But it turns out that the Big "T" truth is that you aren't ever going to know everything. I really knew this to be true when I walked into Pacific University to be an adjunct teacher and kept hearing about the Acceptance and Commitment Therapy model from the students. I thought, "That's weird. I was trained on all the models and I haven't heard of this one... ugh." The Acceptance and Commitment Therapy model came out when I was out of grad school and I was working. I hadn't been keeping up with what was current in my field. Argh. Need to start working on that too. (Cue imposter syndrome music.)

You have your own soundtracks for things happening in your world, right? I have my "badass music," my "sad music," my "I'm-feeling-awesome music," my "things-are-changing music," and of course, my "failure music." If you don't have yours picked out yet, next time things are happening in your world, settle into your chair and think about your life as a movie. What music would be playing as you make this choice or do this thing? It is pretty awesome; maybe not life-changing, but a quick and easy way for me to check in with myself and see what is happening. Pro tip!

For example, my husband and I just moved. And during the process the soundtrack for that move was from *The Lord of the Rings Trilogy* where we watch the characters run across New Zealand (I mean Middle-earth) for–ev–er. My move felt like every painstaking moment of those scenes. Don't get me wrong—I love *The Lord of the Rings* and *The Hobbit*—but some of those scenes. I mean, really, they were *so* long.

When I think about imposter syndrome, it's like hearing someone else's theme music in my head for what I am doing. I feel like the song should be familiar, but it's not. It is scary to sit with this feeling. It's scary to wonder if I am going to get caught or if I am going to fall into something headlong and not get out.

The fear of not doing it well, not being enough, not being what the other person wants is palpable. It is so real. Even when the boss says "Yep. Looks about right. Good job." Or my clients walk out of my office saying, "That really hit home today." Or there are people whose lives are changed because of what I am doing, I still think, "If they only knew. I don't know what I am doing; I am making this up as I go."

It's easy to mistake not knowing everything for being an imposter. But you are not an imposter. You are afraid of disappointing someone, of proving the little "t" truth in the back of your mind that you aren't enough. No amount of extra knowledge, no degree is going to give you enough information to dampen that fear. We deal with that fear by realizing that we have what we need to be what is needed for this situation. We have the tools of problem-solving, making choices, and being flexible with the things that get thrown at us. The more we recognize that we are enough and can handle whatever comes our way, the easier it is to navigate through these fears. If we are willing to wrestle with our fears and sit with our authentic selves—on purpose, with intention—we will find imposter syndrome doesn't feel as overwhelming as it did before.

Chapter 8: A French Fry Shaped Hole in Your Heart

To accept something, does not mean you like it.
It means you know you can't change it.
It means you know you need to find another way.
It means you know it is time to let go.
It means you know it is time to move on.
It means you are ready to discover what is next.
Are you ready?

Thom Rutledge

One day at the residential treatment facility where I worked, I witnessed a moment between a staff member and a client that was mind-blowing. Life changing. Reality testing. The young woman was sitting at the table with the staff member and was piling French fries on to her plate. She looked as if she was planning to take every last one of the massive pile (we prepped food for 14 people every night, so lots and lots of fries). My staff member said, "It looks like you are trying to eat some of your feelings. What's really going on?" Kiddo just said, "Nothing. I am just hungry." Staff said, "I know your mom didn't show up today for her visit—could this be sadness that you are trying to make go away by French fries?" Kiddo got teary-eyed and just kept eating. The staff member said, "Go ahead and take as many fries as you think it will take to fill that hole in your heart." The girl did, and they sat together at the table while she ate them. At the end of the pile with the last fry in her mouth, my staff said, "How's the hole? Did that work?" And the girl sobbed even more and said no. They sat together through the tears and the young woman shared her disappointment with the staff and wept for her loss. My staff supported her and they moved through this pain together.

How many French fries does it take to feel better? How did we get to this place where we believe French fries, alcohol, or those damn

Reese's peanut butter cups are going to solve whatever problem we are having? We distract, we bury, we run away from, we ignore. We don't sit with uncomfortable-ness well. We want to make it go away quickly, so we find the easiest solutions, the solutions where we can be in control.

We don't spend a lot of time learning how to sit with uncomfortable-ness in our own soul. When an uncomfortable feeling rises in us, we immediately want to try and find a way to get rid of it. We try to distract ourselves with over-committing or avoid it by being busy or binging. We attempt to hide from the feelings by analyzing or explaining it enough. The little "t" truth here is that that will get us back to a state of "okay-ness" which is better than sitting in the pain. The big "T" truth is we need to start to be okay with sitting in the uncomfortable feeling and process through it. Which may mean grieving the loss of our expectation, allowing the frustration to be real and allowing ourselves to grow from it.

Sadness, frustration, grief, pain are not things to be feared, run from, buried, or ignored. They are important elements to making sure we are present. Making sure we are intentional and living our full lives.

So how do we disconnect our French Fry Coping skill and learn to sit with our discomfort? As people pleasers, we know how to sit with discomfort for the benefit of others. The question is, can we sit through discomfort for ourselves? Sitting with discomfort is important and valuable and a great learning opportunity. We just don't like to do it. We can convince ourselves that doing it for others is noble, right, selfless—but sitting through discomfort for ourselves is selfish; we are wasting time on something that will only benefit us so we should "fix" it as fast as we can by using the quickest tool possible so that we can get back to helping others. Sound familiar? Or do you just think, "That feeling just sucks and I don't want to feel that way so I just want to get rid of it?" That's familiar too.

One of the benefits of sitting with discomfort is being able to make more intentional choices. Let's say every time you were sad, a large McDonald's fries appeared in your hand. You ate them all (most often not intentionally!) and you gained weight and then struggled with your appearance. Is using that tool (French fries) to solve your problems really working for you? Are those French fries really filling that hole in your heart? Is eating fries really a way to make good on your goals? Are you able to do eat non judgmentally in the long run? Nope.

Another benefit of sitting with your discomfort is finding the lesson it is trying to teach. How can you learn the lesson of failure, or trouble, or sadness, or rage if you are covering it up with a mountain of fries? (Or really, if I am honest, a bag of Ruffles and some white chocolate Kit Kat's. Damn those Hershey folks.)

Why is learning the lesson important? Well, because if we don't learn it here, we will have to learn it somewhere. Why not here? Why not now? Learning these lessons are building blocks to a successful future. Think about if we never learned how to tie our shoes. We would also never be able to tie a bow for packaging, or tie a knot so the things in a POD don't go flying all over the place when we move! We would never be able to secure almost anything with rope. And what good would that do us on a stranded island with Wilson? We couldn't build a shelter in the Zombie apocalypse. Problems abound when we don't learn the lessons.

What lesson are you avoiding today? Is it fear-based? Sadness-based? Anger-based? Think back to times you were offered an opportunity to learn the lesson and skipped it. What coping skill did you use to skip it? Is it similar (or exactly the same) as the one you are using now?

Using the O in S.O.B.E.R. is how we disconnect our coping skills and learn to sit with our uncomfortableness. Observe what is happening both inside and outside of you in the situation. By observing you get the opportunity to really sit with and lean into your emotions and give yourself a chance to learn from the situation. It is uncomfortable, yes, but leaning in helps you grow.

Chapter 9: Brokenness

> What lies behind us and what lies before us are tiny matters compared to what lies within us.
>
> *Ralph Waldo Emerson*

Failure. Brokenness. Hopelessness. The feeling that life circumstances can never get back to where they were. There is some truth in that. When something has changed, we can never go back to where it was. It is vital that we adjust your expectations. That we work through the grief and allow ourselves an opportunity to change.

A picture I found on the wide internets shows a bowl that is cracked and broken with gold running along the cracks. The image is captioned: In Japan, broken objects are often repaired with gold. The flaw is seen as a unique piece of the object's history, which adds to its beauty. Consider this when you feel broken.

Everything in life changes us. Grows us, makes us. Some things crack off a piece. Some things scar. Some things create and grow. Each element creates something awesome and unique about us as individuals, as families, as a collective. As we interact and grow, we impact each other too.

Transitioning our mindset (in Cognitive Behavioral Therapy we call it Cognitive Restructuring and Reframing) helps us to think about things differently and allow that opportunity to become truth. When I look at something that is broken, I think, "It's trash now. It's worthless." When I reframe it, I can look at the same broken thing and think, "This has a new history—a new story about it." It becomes something charming and emotionally charged.

When I think about the times I have made mistakes and have let those mistakes define me, I feel gross, icky, and a downright failure. As a perfectionistic person, I have often carried those mistakes with me for years. Things that were small when they happened... and frankly are small now. Earlier I shared a story of a friend who gave me gold hoop earrings and I was unintentional with my words. Those words hurt a friendship. I am still working on repairing that brokenness with gold. A recent example is a little "t" truth that I am terrible with money. When the actual facts are there have been times I thought I paid a bill and I didn't. Which meant I owed a late payment. None of those mean I am terrible with money. Just that I made a mistake. But in my brain I perseverate on the missed payment and feel like I must learn everything I can about budgeting so I never make that mistake again. When I can reframe those same mistakes and think about what I have learned—and even think about who I would be if I didn't make that mistake—I find that my life wouldn't be the same. I don't know that it would have been better or worse if I hadn't made that mistake; I do know that I wouldn't have these new stories. These new unique marks.

Brokenness doesn't have to be life ending. It can be a new beginning with a history.

The transition from the mistakes I have made to acceptance and acknowledgment of those new unique marks was hard. The shift takes time and patience and sitting with uncomfortable feelings. It takes sharing those feelings with others and asking for what you need. It takes being open to learning lessons and taking baby steps towards the reframe. Often I have clients who are struggling with depression or feeling so anxious that they just feel like there is no chance for them to have or do anything better than this. They wonder if this feeling will last forever. Forever? No. It won't last forever. But when you are in the midst of brokenness, you feel like it will never get any better. You feel like it will last forever. When I start working on reframing with clients, I often try to help them recognize that the end goal is not necessarily the opposite of the thoughts they are having, but a more accurate representation of the big "T" truth.

I believe in reframing because sometimes we just need to take control of what we believe. We need to teach our brain the truth. Reframing can absolutely help us transition our thoughts from one place to another. I think sometimes we want this to be instantaneous. Which is why we give up quickly when we don't see results. We also struggle because we leap too far from what we are willing to believe. If we go from "I'm fat and ugly" to "I'm just right and beautiful," we might not be willing to make the leap that quickly. What if we started with an approximation, just a little closer to our goal statement, than we are today? "I'm working on my weight and I love my eyes." This reframing might be easier to swallow than the whole kit and caboodle. When clients share with me that they are feeling broken and too far gone to save or help, I start with an approximation of where they are wanting to go and offer them a reframe like, "You have found yourself in a vulnerable spot, you are ready to move forward." I am not telling them that they are going to be a gold-laden bowl in two weeks. I *am* saying we are ready to pick up the pieces. Approximation gives us time to move closer to the truth in a slow and steady way that is easier to believe.

Brokenness is a state of transition. It moves us to the next place. Sometimes we have to be broken to move forward in a new and different way. Brokenness belongs on my "I do not think it means what you think it means" list. Brokenness isn't final. It is a thing that happens, and we decide how we move on from it.

Chapter 10: Justifying your decisions

> Every positive change in your life begins with a clear, unequivocal decision that you are going to either do something or stop doing something.
>
> *Unknown*

When I make a decision that doesn't fit in with what is expected of me (little "t" truth), I find myself feeling the need to apologize or justify my decision. I feel like people won't understand the decision or would judge me for my choice.

I realized the other day that not everyone has this issue. I thought everyone had this internal push, pit of their stomach, need to explain their decision-making process or give an explanation or excuse when they have to say no or make a decision. Turns out, it's just us, reader. Just us. As I have been writing this book, I have found myself apologizing, explaining, and making excuses for all sorts of things. I have been really challenged by this in my editing process. I don't think I even noticed that I was doing it until I was working to be intentional with everything in the book. As I started to look at things intentionally, I realized I don't need to explain why I like honey-lemon water and not coffee or tea. I don't need to apologize or make an excuse for why I don't shave my legs every day. But wow, did I have long-winded justifications throughout the book that have now been removed!

Sometimes we are faced with this feeling of necessity to do the right thing. And interestingly enough, the right thing is always what someone else wants or needs. And it is rarely, if ever, what we want or need. We ask questions of each other on the most boring and basic of topics to make sure we are making the other person happy, instead of sharing our desires and working together to work out what to do. But compromise and working together can be just as fulfilling as conceding to the other person's desires.

Think of the last time someone asked you to do something and you had other plans. Your first thought was, "How can I do both?" I know. Your next thought was, "Oh goodness. I am going to disappoint someone. What can I say that will make it seem worth it to cancel or say no? Or to sound like it is not my fault?" Or your thought might be, "Who did I disappoint last time, so I don't do that again?" A whirlwind swirls in your mind as you try to figure out how to make everyone happy—without checking in on what you really want to do.

I hear you; you said the "S" word. I know, I know you did! You said, "That is selfish."

Is it? No. Checking in with yourself to see what you want to do is not selfish. Demanding that your friends only do what you want to do all the time or creating unrealistic expectations of what others are able to do in your life is selfish. But checking in with yourself and making sure your needs are met too? Not selfish. Remembering that it is not either their needs or mine, there is a "both/and" that can be identified. Both needs are important, and we may need to determine which is the priority right now—not whose needs are more important.

When we give an explanation for something (turning down an event or invitation) we are not allowing our "yes" to be yes, and our "no" to be no. We are not allowing our intentional choice to answer the question with what we want to be enough. If someone wants a reason why they can ask for one. Your reasons may not be anyone else's information. If I don't want to go swimming because I am struggling with my weight and how I look in a swimsuit, that is not a reason I need to give anyone. I can just say, "No thanks." Even typing those words my fingers flew into a frenzy of wanting to write other socially acceptable reasons for not going swimming. This a lesson I just keep learning.

We often feel because of our upbringing/culture/religion/anxiety—or any myriad combinations—that in order to be polite we must give a reason for our actions when they don't fit what we see as the expected behavior. And what we see as the expected behavior is taking care of others' needs regardless of our needs. But here is the kicker: Sometimes the social norm is not accurate, not acceptable, or not okay. These social norms are really just things that groups of people agree with for a period of time, and sometimes they change from week to week. So it is a little "t" truth. It is an opinion, and as we know, opinions are not fact and do not have to be treated as such. People following these opinions as big "T" truths will struggle from societal whiplash between what they think should be happening and what really is happening.

I think we confuse the social norm of being polite with our interpretation of it. We believe that we are being polite when we say "yes" to events we don't want to go to for fear of hurting other people's feelings. We believe we are being polite when we agree in order to make the other person happy. And we believe we are being polite when we give reasons for why we are doing things or not doing things. And If I'm not being polite, I am rude, which means people won't like me and I won't be good enough. But what if our beliefs about what is polite are wrong? If we are looking at these things as big "T" truths when they are actually just our opinions or little "t" truths?

The big "T" truth is, you can say "no" with no other explanation and not be rude. You don't have to give an explanation unless you a) want to, or, b) they ask you. (And even then, you don't actually have to give a reason at all if you don't want to. And that is still not rude). No one needs your explanation. You will need to check in with yourself (yep, I said it again) and see if you want to give an explanation. If you don't—don't.

"No" is enough.

I sat with a client who was feeling guilty about a sexual encounter she had engaged in. We discussed her situation and at one point I said, "This wasn't your fault. You didn't need to give him a reason why you didn't want to have sex. 'No' is enough." That was a lightbulb moment for her and for me. "No" is enough. She didn't owe him anything else. And neither do I. I don't owe the world an explanation for my weight, for why I moved, for what I am doing with my life. I am enough as I am and if I want to say "no," no is enough.

"No" is a complete sentence. Learning to use the word *no* as a complete sentence is tough, especially when people are coming out of a co-dependent relationship and are re-learning how to be individuals. We want to explain to others what we are thinking and feeling out of politeness, but we also just want to be understood. We want to know that the other person gets us and is okay with what we have going on. But the truth is, some people are not ever going to get us and what we say. You know who they are, the folks for whom your explanation never seems to be good enough. They always have a reason why they should be able to pursue an activity or attend an event, and why you should be able to join them. To them, it is never just okay for you to be you and make your choices. The other people in your life are probably fine with a "no" and no explanation—but there are those choice few, right?

Not everyone needs an explanation—everyone does need an answer. You checking in with yourself and knowing what answer you want to give is vital.

How do you do that? How do you check in with yourself when what you have going on is usually fear-, guilt-, shame-, courtesy-, or politeness-oriented? Let's look at this from the same perspective as we did your S.O.B.E.R. skills. The two extremes in the "examine your options" part of the skill would be "my needs don't matter and my needs are the only ones that matter." The part that will feel just about right would lie somewhere in between. It might look like giving yourself permission to think about yourself as equally important with the other person. In order to do that, you have to know what you actually want, instead of what you think will make the other person feel good or what will work in this situation. Take off that "selfish" mantle and just ask, "Do I (for no other reason that it would be awesome) want to..." whatever it is? If the answer is "yes," use your S.O.B.E.R. skills figure out how you will do it with no judgment, fully present, and on purpose. If your choice is to say "no," say no and do what you can do with no judgment, fully present, and on purpose. Be intentional about how you spend your time—you only have so much of it. It is always lovely to give time to friends, be with your partner, and do things for your kids, so make it an intentional gift. Make sure you are fully present the whole time.

Chapter 11: Apologizing

> Our job is not to deny the story, but to defy the ending - to rise strong, recognize our story, and rumble with the truth until we get to a place where we think, Yes. This is what happened. This is my truth. And I will choose how the story ends.
>
> *Brene Brown*

Let's talk about "I'm sorry."

I used to say "I am sorry" about everything. Two people in a grocery store down the aisle from me bump into each other, and I say that I am sorry. I wasn't even involved! What the heck? "I am sorry" has so many sub contexts....

- I am embarrassed.
- I am not enough.
- I shouldn't have these feelings.
- I shouldn't have done this thing.
- I am too much.
- I am not okay.
- You are likely embarrassed so I should feel your pain with you.

When are good times to say you are sorry? There are two different types of actual "I am sorry." One is when you actually messed up. And another is when you feel bad about what someone else is going through.

When we apologize because we have done something wrong, the apology can often bring a small sense of relief that we have started to make amends. When we apologize because someone is feeling pain and we empathize, we feel connected to the other person. When we apologize for something that is actually a sub context—we are embarrassed, for instance—the apology often makes us feel worse;

we feel more shame and more guilt. It doesn't make us feel any better. It isn't giving us the resolution because we aren't addressing the original feeling.

Apologizing is okay. We can say we are sorry for lots of reasons. Our struggle most often is that we need to learn to apologize correctly—when we need to—not just as a comma or an acknowledgment of embarrassment. It is one hundred percent okay for me to not apologize to those people who hit each other in the grocery store aisle. It is not my fault, and though I feel embarrassed for them, I don't need to apologize for that either. It is okay to just feel that uncomfortable feeling and move on. There's the crux of it: I felt uncomfortable, so I apologized.

When I don't shave my legs in the morning and my husband touches them later in the evening, I apologize to him. He laughs and reminds me I don't need to apologize. As I look at it now, I realize that it is because I am embarrassed. I am worried I am not enough and I am struggling to find a way to make sure he is comfortable. So I apologize. And I haven't done anything wrong (by not shaving)! I am apologizing for being embarrassed (sub context), so I don't end up feeling better. Yuck.

When I write all that out and think about it, I realize that I am not allowing myself to take up as much space as what I am giving to others. Would I do that to anyone else? Would I limit their space to be in a relationship with me? Nope. I would absolutely open up and offer them space and be a participant in our relationship. I need to do that for myself too. I need to facilitate an opening for myself to make sure I am a part of the relationship and in doing so, I need to honor my choices.

I chose not to shave today, I feel fine about that, until it infringes on my husband. (And just to be clear, it is my interpretation that my not shaving infringes on him! It is actually not true at all. I just make it up in my head!) When I feel like it impacts my husband, I start to feel guilty. When I dig deeper into that I realize it is because I wonder if I am being a good wife if I am not taking care of my body (another little "t" truth; taking care of my body must mean that I shave my legs every day). So I have to dig into that. Where did that little "t" truth come from? As I dig in, I realize more and more that there is not an *actual* reason to feel guilty, embarrassed, or sorry for not shaving my legs.

My mom has a quote in her email signature that says: "Three Pieces of Advice: never waste the opportunity to tell someone you love them; never take the credit or the blame for something you didn't do, and always tell the truth, it's easier to remember."

All three of these really resonate with me. The one that I want to focus on right now is the second one. Not taking the credit comes easily to me. I struggle to take the credit for things I have done! But the second half—don't take the blame for something you didn't do—that is a little harder. As we apologize for the sub context, we take the blame for something that is not our issue. Put into different terms: we are stealing. Just writing that I am stealing something from someone else makes me a little antsy. It makes me feel a little gross. I wouldn't ever steal from someone. Did that make your heart leap with guilt and shame?

Okay, that sounds a little dramatic, but seriously, this is kind of what we are doing. What are we stealing? We are stealing the other person's responsibility, their opportunity to feel their feelings, their stuff. When I apologize for the people in the grocery store, I am robbing them of the opportunity to take responsibility for their actions and hold on to their own discomfort. When I do that and take all the responsibility, I don't give them a chance to grow. I need to own that it's not my stuff.

There it is. Wow. I feel like I say that all the time to clients. Whose stuff is this? If it is not yours, put it down. I realize I sound like I am talking to a five-year-old at this point—but, really! Sometimes we are all totally five years old when we impulsively pick up other people's stuff and try to take it on as if it is our own. It's not yours. Put it down.

Saying "sorry" for things that are not your responsibility reveals your own need to not feel uncomfortable. It is wanting other people to not feel uncomfortable, and it is a struggle. The struggle is real.

So what do we do about it? We have to put it down. When the urge comes to saying you are sorry, practice your S.O.B.E.R. skills. Stop before you say it and ask some questions: What is going on inside of me? What is going on outside of me? What is it that I can do about meeting the internal or external needs? Make your choice: Non judgmentally, on purpose, and fully present. Use your S.O.B.E.R. skills often so you get in the habit of checking in with yourself and make intentional choices. Don't be an impulsive five-year-old.

Recognize that "sorry" is not a polite thing to say when it is not our stuff. It doesn't make things better; it reinforces that we are uncomfortable and that we are not dealing well with the discomfort. We can sit with that discomfort and allow it to teach us. The uncomfortableness allows us to learn something about ourselves and about our reactions. We can find out some interesting things about ourselves when we sit with the discomfort.

Discomfort teaches patience, understanding, grace, and mercy. Discomfort creates growth. Think about the term *growing pains*. (And maybe the show from the '80s!) The term *growing pains* literally indicates that a body is doing something at a rate that is generally faster than it knows how to cope with, and therefore a person experiences a little pain during the growth process. Emotional discomfort, social discomfort, the world not living up to our expectations—these usually don't cause physical pain—but sometimes we do feel them. Discomfort—for those of us who have been attempting to avoid it all our lives—can indicate that we are in a place where we are getting ready to grow. And that can be both scary and really awesome at the same time. It is not actually a terrible thing to experience discomfort while we grow and change. These feelings are just data that help us understand what is going on.

Next time you are uncomfortable, be an archeologist and take your little brush and start sweeping back the dirt and debris to figure out what is underneath. Is it a beautiful shell that is just waiting to be put on display? Is it a Tyrannosaurus Rex that is ready to blow your mind? What could it be?

Chapter 12: Black and White

> Although the world is full of suffering, it
> is also full of overcoming it.
>
> *Helen Keller*

What is black and white and grey all over? Life.

Often people with anxiety tend to believe in the black and white and struggle with grey. Black and white seems to make life simple, and in some situations it does. Murder verses self-defense, right? Murder is wrong. Self-defense is okay. Then it gets all squidgy in the middle where we realize people may murder and call it self-defense. Ummm, let's not go down that rabbit trail. Let's stick to some things that are closer to home. After all, none of *my* readers would be contemplating real murder!

Black and white examples I have heard in therapy:

If I don't go back to college this term, I will never graduate college. I will be a loser all my life.

If I don't get married by 24, I'll be alone forever.

If I buy this house and it is the wrong one, I will be stuck with it forever.

I'll always be anxious.

This will never get better.

Everything is hopeless.

The universe doesn't give a crap about me.

Things never work out for me.

My wife hates me.

And more. But the world isn't really black and white. We make choices—hopefully intentional ones—and then we keep going down the road. I like to think of life as a freeway. But not just any freeway! Have you ever seen an aerial view of the Los Angeles freeway system? It is not Route 66, one long stretch and once you get on there are not many places to turn off, stop, or turn around. In Los Angeles, there is a turn off almost every mile, and every turn off gives you a chance to turn around. During college, I lived near LA and I remember having to have a *Thomas Guide* in the front seat of the car to help me figure out where I was going and how to get back when I took a wrong turn. Thank goodness for a GPS now that can help us do that automagically! But looking at those *Thomas Guide* maps gave me a really clear understanding that every turn I take, every exit off the freeway has a way back to the freeway. And everywhere you go there is another chance to get back on and go either in the same direction or a different one. There is choice after choice. No decision is permanent. But anxiety creates a sense of finality to every decision. It makes us think that if we make any one choice we are rejecting everything else, and we have no way back. Life is not actually like that.

In therapy I talk a lot about choices and intentions. We worry about making the wrong choice. There are good choices, solid choices, scary choices, better choices, worse choices—but I have a hard time with the terms *right* and *wrong* choices. Choices lead you in the direction where you are headed (if you know where you are headed!) And if you don't know where you are headed, the choices won't deter you from the path, they are just an exploration. So if choices are just choices—if there is no right or wrong—then there is just a lot of grey in the middle.

For example, a client was deciding whether or not to go back to college. She said, "If I don't choose now it will cost me $6,000 because they won't refund after today. But what if that is the wrong choice?" We sat with that for a minute and thought about the words. Yes, she could choose not to return today and keep her $6,000. If in two weeks she wanted to go back, she could call the school, apply again, and continue her education next semester. Would she be unable to attend forever? No. Would she be unable to attend this semester? Yes. That would be a choice. That choice would cost her six months of time. She could also go for the first two weeks of class and then choose to leave school and forfeit that $6,000. That would be a choice; that choice would cost her $6,000. Neither are good, bad, or otherwise. They are just choices—choices that she will learn from and pay for no matter what. Is either the right choice? Not really. She doesn't know where she wants to go with life so neither path will take her away from her end goal because she is just exploring right now. Two months from now, six years from now, 20 years from now she can go back to school (that school or any other) and finish up the degree. That would be a choice too. Or she could decide she never wants to go back and do something else with her life. That's another choice.

I like describing black-and-white thinking as a bell curve from statistics class. I don't actually remember a ton about statistics; I do remember correlation does not prove causation. I remember my dissertation math being really difficult for me to understand and I had a wonderful tutor and friend walk me through every piece of it so I could explain it to my committee. But I remember the bell curve well. It stuck with me from the moment I learned about it in my assessments class and looked at all the data on intelligence testing.

The bell curve is a visual representation of a normal distribution of data. I believe that life has an equal number of positive and negative scenarios. The bell curve indicates that most of the scenarios are going to fall within the middle of the chart (grey area), and not at the extremes (black and white).

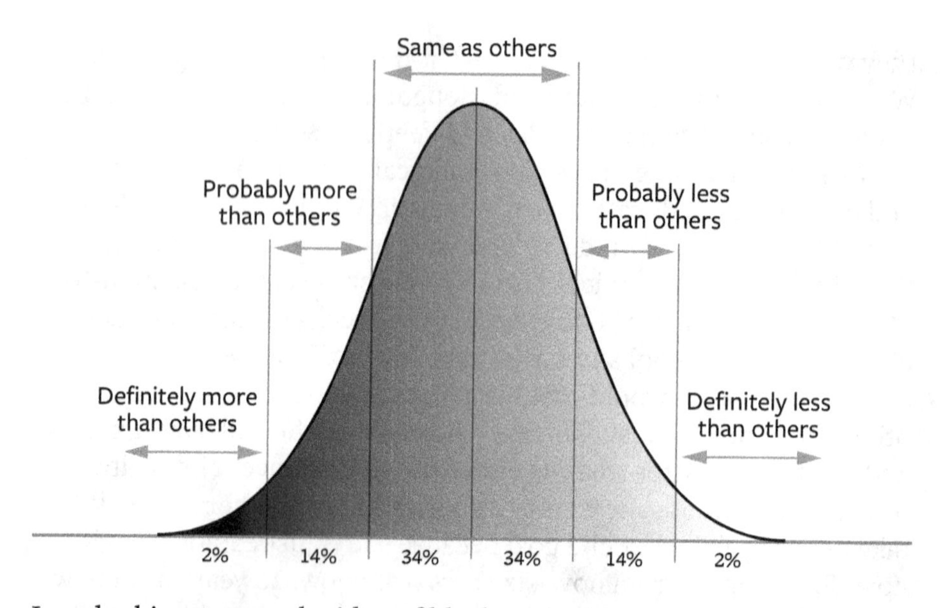

I apply this curve to the idea of black-and-white thinking. If there are only four percent of the possibilities that are *actually* black or white—did you fully stop at the stop sign, did you pay for that? (Yes or no answers)—and 96 percent is in the grey in the middle, then we have to evaluate our big scary questions from the premise that our answer—our truth—is likely in the grey.

Will your wife always hate you? Probably not. There's grey there.

If you buy this house will you have to always and forever keep it? No, you can move or sell it.

Will this ever get any better? Well, there have been times where it was better and more likely than not, it will get better again. There is grey there.

There is always an answer to the question you have and that answer is most likely grey. You may have leanings toward the black or leanings toward the white, but a true black-or-white answer? Probably not. The S.O.B.E.R. skills have us come up with five options as we make an intentional choice. The two extreme options that we find show us those black-and-white ways of looking at things. And tend to help us realize that those extremes are really useful in making a choice we are really okay with. When we spend some time charting out and thinking of the grey responses, we have an opportunity to really move out of our absolutes (which produce fear) and into our possibilities (which produce hope). When we have hope, things are less scary. Hope is a nightlight for our soul.

If we are able to accept that every decision is just that, a decision that can be changed, our anxiety has a much smaller foothold. Anxiety can then try and convince us it was the wrong decision, but if it was, we have a way out. We can change our mind. That's what I mean about murder; it is the one area that once we have chosen it, we can't really take it back. We can be sorry about it, but we can't really change our mind once we have already done it. I use this example a lot.

When I am discussing black-and-white thinking with my clients, sometimes we have to work through multiple scenarios before they realize they have a choice in almost everything. As they present argument after argument where they only feel like there is one option from which to choose, and I come up with alternative after alternative, they start to realize there are a million options. Life is not black and white. We have a *million* options. And all of them have consequences. Not good, bad, or otherwise—just stuff that happens because we chose left and not right. And guess what? We can go right if we want to! Head back and take the other road. Nothing is permanent except murder!

Anxiety and depression tell us we are stuck with whatever decision we have made. That is not accurate. It is a little "t" truth that we believe because we have been convinced it *is* true. I kind of imagine anxiety and depression as creatures winking behind my back when I say that because they know it isn't true too. But they don't share that news with us. We have to be focused and intentional about our choices and about our reactions so that we can recognize the little "t" truth for what it is: the deception of anxiety and depression.

Chapter 13: Boundaries

> Owning our story and loving ourselves through that process is the bravest thing that we will ever do.
>
> *Brene Brown*

Boundaries are essential to survival. One of the first things we did as people was start to define our territory and decide who we keep out and who we allow in. One of the things people pleasers do is give others free rein to our spaces. I describe in therapy that our boundaries are like a home in a neighborhood. We have the inner core of our house (the bedroom) where most people don't go. We have a living room where people we invite inside can gather and share intimate times with us. We have the front porch or back yard where we might host a gathering or two, but inside might be off limits. We have the fence line that keeps people off the private property. Our job is to figure out where people belong. The random guy coming to do a survey doesn't belong in your bedroom. But neither does an overly intrusive mom if you don't want her there. When you have "friends" who have been in your life for 30 years tell you they are "just trying to help" by ripping down things you love or barging in on your hard-earned peace, they need to revisit your boundaries too. Although boundaries themselves are often pretty stationary, where people are allowed to go within our boundaries are more fluid. We can totally have friends that have spent time in our heart of hearts, and if they change—or we do—we you can move them back to the front porch. Just because they have been allowed in a place before doesn't mean they are always welcome there. We are allowed to change our minds and change our responses to things no matter the circumstances.

How can you think through your boundaries? *Know* your boundaries. Where does your property line end? What are deal-breakers in your relationships? What do you want the whole world to know (unprotected social media); what do you want your nearest and dearest to know? How far can your relationships be pushed? If a friend doesn't call, write, or post in five years, where do they fit when you get back together? Some friends can go straight into your heart of hearts again. With others, it may mean you sit on the porch for a while drinking sweet tea until you can reconnect. There are some boundaries you intuit, and boundaries you may not realize exist until someone crosses them. One boundary I can relate to in an instant is being called names. That is not in my wheelhouse. Friends who regularly tease in this way aren't long-term friends for me. I prefer a different type of friendship. These folks live outside my fence. They may occasionally get invited to parties in my backyard, but they don't get to come freely into my world or see my intimate spaces.

Be thoughtful about who you let where. Now that you have thought about your boundaries, it is time to evaluate where people are currently and if that is where you want them to be. Just because they are family or blood doesn't mean they get to be in your bedroom. Your husband, wife, partner, parents, and others are only allowed where you allow them.

Train your monkeys! Or in this case, train the people you love. You may have to train people to deal with your new (or refreshed, or re-determined) boundaries. If your mom has a habit of barging in unannounced, you may have to escort her back to the door and ask her politely to knock. You may have to have an uncomfortable sit down with these folks to help them determine how they would like to respond to these rules. Brene Brown talks about "standing your sacred ground" and not bowing to others' desires, nor lean back into spinelessness. It is easier to stand this sacred ground when you have used your S.O.B.E.R. skills and made your boundary decisions intentionally, when you have analyzed the options and made the boundaries non judgmentally, on purpose, and fully present. You are then able to be clear and honest about your decisions and hold to them. If we got pulled over every time we rolled through a stop sign, we would clearly learn our lesson and stop appropriately. But we don't, so often we roll on through. People in your life are like that too; without boundaries being held, we sometimes will get rolled on over.

Recognize your worth. You are a gift; special, irreplaceable. When you have something like that, where do you keep it? Your most valuable items? You know that thing you would run back into the house for if there is a fire? Where do you keep it? Is it in a fireproof safe? Is it in a secret spot only you know? Most of the time the things that we really value we keep safe by locking them away. In this example of boundaries, we believe that our passport is valuable so we lock it in a safe and we don't copy the key or give away the combo. Right? It is valuable. You are valuable. You don't just hand over your heart, your mind, your soul to whoever comes around. You keep it safe until you trust them. You deserve to be protected from those who might ignore your boundaries.

Healthy relationships have boundaries. Some people in your life may struggle with you setting up boundaries that limit their access to you. Understanding that this may cause some uncomfortable feelings for you and those folks may hit a soft spot in how you like to be with people. Especially when you want people to like you, trust you, come to you with their needs. You may fear they won't like you unless you compromise your boundaries. I'll tell you, a compromise like that leads to resentment. It leads to frustration. It leads to bad feelings and lack of trust. It makes more sense to be yourself and have people in your world that respect your boundaries than to tear down a wall or fence because they want you to. Have you ever had that friend that was always a bit critical, always responded with a "Yeah, but don't you think (insert their opinion here)"? Someone who has taken advantage of you but also given you a lot (especially when you are down)? They seem to have solutions and such good ideas, but they also come with a price. You don't have to get rid of people or cut them out of your life, but these are the people who you want to be really careful around and with whom you make sure your boundaries are clear. They may be the folks who are invited occasionally into your yard, or maybe they are more like Wilson in *Home Improvement* and you just say "Hi-dee-ho neighbor!" over the fence.

Chapter 14: Selfishness

> Nothing ever goes away until it teaches us what we need to know.
>
> *Pena Chodron*

I want to confront the little "t" truths of what we see as selfish and how much room that takes up in our souls. One of the things we get taught from a very young age is not to be selfish. This often starts with learning how to share and then we overgeneralize that to "everything I have must be able to be shared with everyone." Sometimes the lessons may be born out of actual selfishness or a desire for something that isn't ours or not being able to control our impulsivity. We have, since our childhood, started to put many things under the umbrella of selfishness that really aren't selfish. Giving yourself some time to veg watching Netflix probably isn't actually selfish. It is probably healthy after a long day.

Women, especially, get a lot of pressure about not being selfish. We are told that we should put others first, we should serve ourselves last, that we should be the consummate host with no actual needs. But the truth is we *do* have needs! We can get a serving along with everyone else—hell, even first.

The umbrella of selfishness has grown so big and wide that women who decide not to have children have been labeled "selfish." That men who decide to live their life without a spouse have been labeled "selfish." The people who have spoken their truth about their sexuality or gender have been labeled "selfish." What gives, people?

The definition of selfishness is:

1. devoted to or caring only for oneself; concerned primarily with one's own interests, benefits, welfare, etc., regardless of others.
2. characterized by or manifesting concern or care only for oneself

Our actual use of the word covers so much more. In therapy I often hear people say they don't want to be selfish. This comes up, especially when I am asking them about self-care. "Well, I don't want to be selfish, so I just do the little things like read a book on parenting or marriage." Okay. But is that the book you want to read? Does that fill you up and make you your best self?

Why have we decided that being our best self is wrong and selfish? Isn't our best self who we want our kids to be? Who we want our spouse/partner to be? Who we want our neighbors to be? Why wouldn't we be able to be that too?

Selfishness falls to one extreme of the bell curve. What falls to the other? Selflessness: the thing that we all strive for. We have innately decided that selfishness is bad so we want to get as far away from it as possible. "If I am truly selfless, I will be able to provide for everyone and not have any needs. This means I am not a burden on anyone which will mean everything is wonderful." Right?

Did you catch the fear in there? The fear isn't about being selfish, the fear is about being a burden and having people be put out because of our needs.

What do we know about the bell curve? Well, there are only 2 percent of truly selfish things, 2 percent of truly selfless things, and 96 percent of things that fall in the middle with some leanings

Let's play with some examples:

> My kids want to go to summer camp; I want to spend a week in Bali. I book my tickets to Bali.
>
> My partner wants to go to sushi (which I tolerate but don't really like) and I want to go to Indian. I tell him Sushi tonight, Indian next time we go out.

I want to take a ballet class; we are tight on our finances, but I can squeeze just enough out of the budget to cover it.

I am getting up to get some water from the kitchen, I see my spouse's glass is empty and I ask if he wants some.

All of these examples have come from my therapy experiences, and all of them have been labeled selfish at times. My clients' thoughts around their decisions sounded like this:

I shouldn't have booked those tickets to Bali. I am so selfish. My kids deserve to go to summer camp. I shouldn't have taken that opportunity away from them.

I don't have a right to tell him what I want to go out and eat. He works hard; he deserves to eat what he wants to eat. I'll be fine. We'll do the kind I want next time. Compromise is so much better than being selfish.

Taking a ballet class and changing our budget because I want something is so extravagant, I can't possibly commit to it. I'll probably change my mind in a few months, so why commit?

Offering to get water for my spouse is just trying to pull myself toward selflessness because it was selfish of me to get up and get something without asking him.

The thing to remember is that there are *so* many more details to these decisions.

What if I told you that the woman who booked her trip to Bali has children who are three and four years old? Her mother is going to watch them during the trip and is super excited to spend time with them.

What if I told you that the man who wants to eat at Indian works two jobs and drives Uber to pay the bills and his partner works part-time?

What if I told you that the woman who is taking the ballet class is attempting to put some of herself first after an abusive relationship and divorce?

Context matters when deciding whether we are selfish or not. I would venture to say that we are not selfish much of the time. In fact, because we are so worried about being selfish, we tend to live on the "my needs don't matter at all side of the spectrum." Believing that this makes us selfless. I know we think that selflessness is the goal, but the big "T" truth is that life is not really lived in the extremes, the black and whites. It is lived in the grey. I can respect your needs and my needs. By recognizing when we are truly being selfish, we are able to know that we have crossed over into the extremes. The rest of the time we need to start recognizing that we are worthy, interesting, valuable beings who have needs/desires and wants.

I recently started decorating my space again. For a while I got into this very utilitarian "it must have purpose or it doesn't have value" mentality. I didn't have any little tchotchkes around; I didn't have a lot of memorabilia (except pictures of my hubs and me). Everything had a purpose, or at least I thought it did. When we re-did the living room at our old house, I started going to Pinterest for my inspiration and found I was pinning things that were just beautiful. They had no purpose except to be pleasing. I wondered why I had eliminated those from my life. When we were selling our house and staging the home, I bought a bunch of pillows for the bed. After a few mornings of taking them off and putting them on and back and forth, I said to my husband "I hate all these fruffy pillows." He stopped me and said, "You love these pillows; you had pillows like this when we first met. You love all this fruffyness." I immediately rebelled against the thought and said in my head, "Well, that was then and this is now. I want it streamlined and easy." Then I percolated on it for a time and realized, no, I like it looking beautiful and perfect. I like the counters clean and the rooms looking lovely. This makes my heart sing.

Is it selfish to have my home just so? Is it selfish to spend money on things that I think are beautiful? Where does it cross the line? Well, if my family is going to be eating ramen once a day and nothing else for the month, maybe I have fallen a little close to the line. If I choose to sacrifice a little to get something beautiful that makes my heart sing, that's not selfish. It doesn't cross into the definition of actual selfishness.

Starting to evaluate your decisions based on the actual lines will help you find a balance. If it costs others, that falls to the selfishness side. If it costs yourself, that falls to the selflessness side. There really is a *big* area of grey for the rest of it. It is important to find your place on the spectrum and make the choice to be there intentionally. That takes time, energy, and patience—mostly with yourself.

As you get better at finding that balance you will get better at being able to respect your own needs while also respecting the needs of those around you. You will be able to take care of yourself without feeling guilty, or like you are taking things away from other people. You will be ready to recharge and refresh yourself so you can have the energy to make the intentional choices and live the life you want.

Chapter 15: How are you filling your cup?

> I have come to believe that caring for myself is not self-indulgent. Caring for myself is an act of survival.
>
> *Andre Lorde*

When we talk about self-care, we equate it with putting ourselves first. And many of us cringe. We think "Ugh, who am I to put myself first?" Or we fall back on our beliefs about the last being first and the first being last. We desire to put others in front of ourselves because it feels more natural, it feels more appropriate. I'm going to challenge that a little here. Self-care is not about putting ourselves first as much as it is about making sure we have the energy and resources to live our best life. Self-care is less about the value of the person and more about the fullness of your cup.

I think one of the reasons we think of self-care as selfishness is because we often associate self-care with going out and spending lots of money on ourselves (pedicures, massages, haircuts, getting our nails done, etc.). But self-care is way more than that. I think that is why I started using the term "what fills your cup." It isn't about money at all. It is about what makes you feel refreshed and renewed. For instance, I was talking with a client who had been carrying the weight of the world on her shoulders for 20-odd years. When asked what filled her cup she said, "Having nothing to do and being alone." I challenged this with, "Is that because you are exhausted with all the weight and stress you have been carrying? That doing nothing sounds better than doing something and being even more exhausted? Do you feel refreshed, renewed, and rejuvenated after a time of doing nothing?" She answered, "No, I just feel like I wasted time." When did she feel renewed? When she was in the woods with a little mist on her face. When she was at the beach with her toes in the sand, when she was in the garden pulling weeds. When she was outside. She needed to spend some time outside to get something in her cup. She is not selfish for wanting to do things outside or for *needing* to do them any more than a baby is selfish for needing to eat.

When we think about selfishness we end up in a black-or-white battle in our mind. If I take care of myself first, I am selfish. But is it really a black-or-white statement? I don't think so. Filling your cup is no more selfish than putting gas in your tank. You need it to get to the places you are going. Nutritionists and diet aficionados use the phrase "food is fuel" all the time to tell us that what we put in our body is fuel for what we are able to do with our body. A diet filled with donuts will not get us as far as a nutritious diet. We see it all the time in education research; kids who get healthy, regular meals work better and have an easier time than those who don't. So if filling your gas tank and eating good nutrition gets you to your goals, so does filling your personal cup.

What do I even mean by filling your personal cup? I mean doing things that make you feel like your best self. Things that inspire and grow you; things that are interesting, fun, relaxing; things that don't drain you or leave you exhausted (unless its exercise then you are on your own!). What are you doing that makes you excited, interested, and yourself?

When you are doing these things and your cup is full, you are able to do all the other things much more easily. When your cup is empty, even simple things like taking the dog out or dropping something while cooking can exacerbate your stress and bring out a level of anger and frustration unnecessary to the situation. Think about the last time you dropped a spoon while cooking. Did you pick it up and throw it into the sink with some extra force? Did you curse at it and feel like dumping the whole dinner? Or did you put it in the sink and get a new one thinking little about it? I bet if we were to do some digging, the days you got more frustrated were also the days you felt less full in your personal cup, and the days that you just went on with life were the days your cup was full.

Chapter 15: How are you filling your cup?

We talk a lot about introverts and extroverts (we have tests to tell you what you most likely are; see your psychologist today). One of the main gauges is whether or not you get re-charged by being around people or being alone. (Now there are many other facets and there are lots of introverts who like being around people, but follow me for a moment because I want to tie this to filling your cup.) Here's a quick and dirty test: Think about the last time you were in a room with 25 people whom you knew. When the event was over did you leave feeling amped and excited and talking about the cool stuff you chatted about? Or did you leave feeling drained and wishing for a bath and a glass of wine? Extrovert/ Introvert. My point is, this is an example of what fills your cup! Is it selfish to spend time with others because it fills you up? Nope. You realize your gas tank is on empty and you go fill it up so you can keep going. That's all it is.

So let's talk about what fills us up. Sometimes filling my cup comes from time spent with people, other times it might be time spent by myself. Sometimes it is financially motivated (a little retail therapy) or not if I don't have the cash. Sometimes it is people-motivated. Sometimes it is a really good burger. You are the only one who is going to be able to navigate through the definition of "what fills my cup."

Filling your cup is a daily, weekly, monthly, yearly opportunity for you to be your best self. Which is why a massage and wine are not enough. Truth is, you need variety (just like in your diet) and you need to fill up often (just like your car). How much and how often you need to fill your cup depends on what is going on in your life. Just like filling your gas tank depends on how much you are using your car.

How do you know what fills your cup? Start with these questions:

When I _______________:

- How does it make me feel?
- How long does that feeling last?
- What does it do for me emotionally?

- Does it make me grow or feel like I am my best self?
- Do I notice a change in how I react to other things?

As you ask these questions, expand on your answers. Journal about your relationship with these elements. Ask these questions for all the activities you think fill your cup. Another way to figure out what fills your cup might be to ask your loved ones when they notice you are at your best and when you are struggling. They may be able to give you a hint about what fills your cup. As you find things that fill your cup, make a list. You can revisit that list when you notice your cup getting empty.

I have clients who love hiking. Seeing the difference in their outlook on life when they have spent an afternoon journeying on the Pacific Crest Trail or finding some remote lake—they have a fire in their eyes again. They feel like they can do anything. When weeks go by without some time in the woods, they start revisiting their negative thought patterns, start wondering about their worth, start feeling like they might as well just give up. Those folks need to have regular hiking time to fill their cup.

Mine? When I discovered that exercise made me feel like a badass. I was doing Kickboxing right after college—hated it while it was happening—loved the feeling afterward. Later I found that doing an elliptical workout in the morning and challenging myself to do 5 and 10Ks on the elliptical, trying to get in six miles in the morning, getting medals gave me that same feeling. (If you haven't done virtual 5 or 10Ks, give it a try. I love myself some gold-star action and getting a medal for working out is an *awesome* gold star!) So I have that in the morning to fill my cup. But that alone is not enough; I also know I love a clean sink. I love not having dishes in the sink when I leave my house for the day. So I build time into my routine to take care of the dishes in the morning. But it is not just that. I need time to figure out my to-do list in the morning and drink my honey-lemon water. So I build that into my routine.

Chapter 15: How are you filling your cup?

I tell my clients that routines are not—capital *NOT*—a bad thing. Everyone has them and as you are growing up and learning to adult you will need them. Maybe your parents had a chore list for you. Maybe there were gold stars on it (not saying mine had that at all). Your parents were trying to teach you a routine. They were trying to help you build a foundation for success today. As a grown up, you need that. My watch provides me timelines every day (not sure how I lived without it). Every day it goes off at 6:15 a.m. and says, "Get up." At 6:30 it says, "Dishes," at 7:00 it says, "Set intention." At 7:30 it says, "Workout." At 8:30 it says, "Breakfast." At 9:00 it says, "Shower" and at 10:00 it says to leave for work. Does that sound too regimented? Maybe. I want to reframe it for you, these alarms are a gentle nudge to keep me on track with my plans for the day. They are not hard and fast rules. When it is 7:30 and I am still working on my planner, I can make an intentional choice to push off working out for 10 more minutes if I want to. My goal is not to blindly follow the alarms, it is to help me make intentional choices about my day. And when I follow this schedule, I complete my morning fuel-up. I spend time in a way that makes my day the best it can be.

In order to keep my cup filled throughout the day I need text and phone check-ins with my husband. For many years we worked together at the same company. I miss working with him and seeing him every day at work. Having texts and phone calls helps me stay connected. I also need phone calls with my grandma and time with people that aren't my clients. As a psychologist, the rest of my day is a little more scattered: people coming in and out with appointments. Leaving work and commuting home for dinner and some Netflix time with the hubs. Sometimes I have more work to do so during my intention time the next day I schedule in time to get that done. This structure ensures that my cup always has plenty in it. There are other things that fill my cup too; I am a servant at heart. I love making lunches, coffee, dinner for my husband. I love hosting parties and doing fun gifts and things for friends. I love being in control and making sure the laundry gets done the way I want it done.

Earlier we listed out some self-care items. You worked hard creating that list of things that are important to filling your cup. You may have struggled to join me in believing this was important, but you did it because it *is* important (and you are really good at following directions).

Now we are going to look at pleasure, fun, just-for-the-sake-of-it things. These are things we love not because they produce, or have purpose, but just because. Play is a building block of social relationships. Developmental psychologists describe play as a learning tool that children use to develop and learn societal rules and norms. It is a facilitating piece of our psyche. Play and having fun are important elements of our continued development and our pursuit of peace, happiness, and fun. Play brings joy into our life.

So, what do you do for fun? I love laser tag, skee ball, bowling. I love dancing. I love reading. I love Pinterest. I love board games and getting a pedicure. I love looking at puppies and tiny things.

Why are these things important? If life is filled with only purpose-driven activity or meaning, we will ultimately feel like we are worthless if what we are doing doesn't have meaning or purpose. As overachievers and results-oriented folks, a few minutes of downtime where we are not completing a task can feel like a waste of time. It can feel like we didn't produce so we weren't using it meaningfully. If we weren't meaningful with our time, then maybe we aren't meaningful which then raises the question, "Am I enough if I am not doing something?"

The answer to that question is "yes." Yes, you are enough even if you are not doing anything. You are enough no matter what. And you are so enough that you are able to spend time just breathing, playing, doing or being whatever you want. Wanting to get stuff done is not a problem. You can be busy and get things done on a regular basis. If what you are doing is trying to produce the answer, "I am enough today because I got my to-do list done," then we need to tweak the measurement stick. You are enough today because you *exist.*

Chapter 16: Hustling and overproducing

> Authenticity is the daily practice of letting go of who we think we're supposed to be, and embracing who we are.
>
> *Brene Brown*

I don't think I realized how intertwined the idea of hustling and overproducing was with feeling worthy and being valued until a client of mine talked about it. She talked about having the need to overproduce in order to feel good about what she had done. But in that overproduction, she was spending time away from the things she really valued (her family). She used the example that her boss was asking her to create a "Corolla" by Friday and she was trying to put out an "Escalade." Even though that is not what her boss asked for, it would truly be the best thing and she would feel good standing behind it. She also knew that in order to produce an "Escalade" she would need to work all weekend and not spend time with her kids. She asked the question, "What's it worth to me, to others? If I produce an "Escalade" what will that do for me, my job, my boss? What will that cost me and my children?" All important questions.

From a young age, I did extra credit. In fact, I have a strong memory of doing a book report on parrots over one summer, cover page and all. I always wanted to be thought of as responsible, an overachiever, and someone the teacher could rely on. When I look back on it now, I remember getting that warm fuzzy feeling of being the good kid. I remember owning that status and still caring about what my peers thought about me. I was careful to draw the line between the teacher's pet and someone the teacher could trust to collect things or lead the class. That warm, fuzzy feeling sometimes gets named "people-pleasing." And maybe that is so, but I find it to be a different feeling than that. When I think of people-pleasing I think about wanting to make sure that others want for nothing, that they are happy and getting what they want. But that doesn't really give me the same warm fuzzy as when a teacher picks me, when my boss can't think of anyone better for the job, when I am the "go-to gal" for whatever project it is.

When my client talked about producing an "Escalade" when the boss asked for a "Corolla," my heart panged. I knew what she was talking about. How many times have we put so much effort and energy into something because we thought it needed our best? Because our best was the important part. Because it felt good to have stood behind the "Escalade" and said, "What you asked for was not enough. Here is what is enough." Most often, I wasn't doing so from a place of pride, I was doing so from a place of needing recognition.

My client said, "And I know my boss won't even say thank you for the 'Escalade'. She might not even notice." Uff-da! Right? I mean it would meet her value to put out the "Escalade," but it wouldn't meet the mark of what the boss wanted her to do. The cost is too great.

Think of all the times you have been hustling to produce, trying to build up the right things, do the right things, exceed expectations. Developing a reputation for going above and beyond. Being an A+ gold-star student. If you go back and examine the cost of those endeavors, what did you miss? What was the going rate of your feeling that warm fuzzy? Did it cost you family? Time? Money? Experiences?

As people pleasers, anxious folks, those who struggle with being enough. We have sometimes built an entire life around making sure others are happy, making sure we do the right thing, and making sure that everyone likes us. We often will only choose the paths that allow for others to be happy. We don't give room to know what we like or do what we like because it seems more important to make sure others are happy. In the example of my client, she wanted her boss to be happy so she did more than was asked to ensure it.

Chapter 16: Hustling and overproducing

For more than ten years I worked at an agency that gave me warm fuzzies up the wazoo for being an overacheiver. The warm fuzzies weren't always from management. Sometimes they were from the staff, the people I surrounded myself with, friends I developed over time, the community, the oversight organization. But I got a lot of incremental warm fuzzies. I did good work at that agency and I don't regret the experience and the work I did. But the cost was great. For more than ten years I didn't go back to my hometown more than a couple times to see my family. I missed out on more than ten years with my grandmother. I didn't make time to really develop good friendships; most of mine were born out of a trauma bond in hard work. The cost was great. Recognizing the cost on my family, my physical body (I put on a good 80 pounds during that time), and my money. I know now that I have to ask different questions of where I spend my time, what I do with my life, and then make sure that the warm fuzzy is worth the effort I put in. Making an intentional choice.

Can I do that bit extra and get the recognition? Is it okay to produce an "Escalade?" Sure it is. You may have noticed that I have kind of a "there are no wrong choices (except murder)" theme in this book. This is no different. The problem is not doing too much, nor is it trying to get that warm fuzzy feeling. The problem is making a choice that is not intentional and not realizing the true cost of it, or having unrealistic expectations of what the result will be. Doing something over the top nice for my husband is just fine, as long as I am choosing to do it and am weighing the cost, not doing it because I owe it to him, or because I am worried that he will think I am not good enough if I don't over produce. It is important to be present and in the moment. To intentionally choose to pay that cost instead of haphazardly paying it because you weren't paying attention or you weren't active in the process of choosing. (Keep practicing your S.O.B.E.R. skills!)

Chapter 17: Staircase Coping skills

> Vitality shows not only in the ability to persist but the ability to start over.
>
> *F. Scott Fitzgerald*

As we grow up, we are presented with problems. We have to find a solution, and when we do, we create a neural pathway that helps us remember this is how we solved this problem. So then a new problem is presented, and we start trying to solve that problem with the solution we already found. Sometimes it works (which strengthens the neural pathway) and sometimes it doesn't (which then indicates we need to find a new solution.) When we find that new solution, we create a new neural pathway and we now have two coping skills. (Did you just hear the Count from Sesame Street? Or was that just me?) We continue on this pathway and build coping skill after coping skill which we can then use to help us with more and more problems.

I often talk about building coping skills with my clients. I like to talk about it as a staircase. Each stair represents a way we can respond to a problem. The first few stairs are our most basic responses to problems: Cry out for help. Fight/Flight/Freeze.

The next few stairs depend on how we solved problems in our growing up years. We could have asked for help politely, we could have ignored the problem and it went away, we could have lied, and so on.

The next few stairs increase in solution building. Maybe we solved the problem on our own with strength or cunning, or we outsmarted the issue. Drugs, withdrawal, or food may have been coping mechanisms.

But we just keep building stairs. As we get older, we have 40 to 50 stairs that we use to solve almost any problem. As we build those stairs on things that give us confidence, we are more likely to believe that we can solve any problem. As we build those stairs on things that tear down confidence, things we think are "luck, out of my control, or because I am a bad person or not worth it," we worry more that we won't be able to handle what is next and those coping skills become a bit shaky.

Coping skills stairs are impacted by our decisions. When we are doing all the things that make life great—sleeping well, having a good routine, eating well, drinking enough water, having time for friends and things we love (keeping our cup full)—we have easy access to the top level of stairs. These top levels are our more advanced "adultier" skills. These give us support and help us keep going at our best. When we are under stress, don't get enough sleep, or are making poor choices with food and drink, we have less access to those top levels and tend to fall back to our reactive basic responses to problems.

When you have filled your cup by getting up on time, showering, and having breakfast—and then drop your coffee. You might just take a few deep breaths, say, "Dang it..." clean it up, and move on. No harm, no foul.

What happens when you have not kept your cup full (you have overslept, missed your alarm, and the shirt you wanted to wear to work was wrinkled and gross)—and you drop your coffee? You yell, or you cry, or you just sit in a lump. Fight, flight, or freeze.

The coping skills you use when you're feeling at your best are much harder to access when you are overwhelmed, but in the moment it is hard to realize this. When we are stressed we fall back on the less effective skills we learned earlier in life. When this happens we start to question ourselves, "why can't I handle this?", "I should know better, why did I overreact?" or "Why do I always fall back to drinking? I know I need to stop."

The best way to deal with this is to keep our cup full. However, even when we are doing everything we can to stay full, sometimes life drains our cup for us. At these times we can recognize that we are less likely to use our best skills. These are times when we may need to ask for help from those around us, or at least be very aware that we will need recognize when we are tempted to just react, and make an intentional decision instead.

When I go through this activity with clients we work on recognizing our need to give ourselves some grace and admit that we are not at the top of our stairs some times. Whether by our own actions or the things life throws at us. When we notice that and *Stop* what we are doing to give us a chance to *Observe* what is going on inside and outside of us we take realistic stock of what coping skills we have to use at this time. When we know that we are able to *Breathe* and *Examine the Options* that are actually available to us. If we don't have the options available to us that we usually rely on (like sitting down and meditating or doing a pro and con list) because the stress is too great – we don't have to beat ourselves up over it, we just accept we are at a different spot in the stair case and make a choice that we have access to. We *Respond* with *no judgment at ourselves, being fully present and on purpose.* Being intentional in our reaction (instead of our base reaction) allows us the confidence that we can figure out problems and survive any situation.

Chapter 18: Consequences

Well, well, well, if it isn't the consequences of my own actions.
Unknown

One of my favorite elements of learning about behaviorism was learning about consequences. Consequences are the end result of an action. They are neither good or bad, they are just are. Culturally we often throw the word *consequences* at actions that are bad and say things like: "Actions have consequences" (usually in a mean or negative tone – Read: little "t" truth).

But the big "T" Truth is *all* actions have consequences. We see this in science (probably in physics which I didn't take because it was not required when I was in school). Something about "actions have equal and opposite reactions"—I am sure my editor will help me put actual words in this section that make me sound smart. (Or, more likely, my husband will put a footnote in this section and clarify all the science-y stuff.[4] Thanks, honey.)

But when science talks about this, it is not saying we *shouldn't* move stuff, or that we *should* move stuff. It is saying that *if* we move stuff, there will be a result. It is the same with all the choices we make in life. It is not a matter of we should or shouldn't take an action, it is important to understand that when we take an action there is a consequence. It is also important to understand that deciding not to take action is a choice as well and follows this same rule. Not doing something has consequences too.[5]

---

4 He says, "Newton's Third Law of Motion."

5 He says, "If you still have questions about this concept, listen to the song 'Freewill' by Rush."

When you work out, you sweat. You build muscles or cardiovascular health—those are consequences to your actions. When you eat too much food from fast food restaurants (all week because you are stressed about your move; we have talked about my emotional eating), you gain weight. Consequences stem from choices. That's it.

This action equals that reaction.

When you yell at your partner, they may get their feelings hurt. When you push too hard toward getting everything done on your to-do list, you miss out on the fun things that are going on. And you made those choices... either intentionally or not.

Actions have consequences in black-and-white-and-grey-all-over ways! It is important to understand this concept when we use our S.O.B.E.R. skills. As you are evaluating your options, you need to think about the consequences of each option, think through which option is going to have the intended consequences.

When we make sure to spend time *Observing* our situation (both inside and out) we have an opportunity to get clear and put things in perspective. Once we know the real situation (not just our perception of it based on our little "t" truths) we are then able to *Examine the Options*. When we are looking at options we can decided what options will have the *consequences* that we are looking for and which ones have consequences we are wanting to avoid. Our goal is not only to try to get to the consequences we want, but to be able to make the decisions based on our ability to sit with the consequences that happen. Non-judgmentally, fully present and on purpose.

When I have this conversation with clients, it usually stems from their comment that they can't (or have to) do something. They don't usually recognize the choices that they have. They might say "I never have enough time for myself because I have to make dinner for the family every night." Do they *have* to make dinner every night? Nope. There are lots of options to how to have dinner every night. You can order in, you can have a delivery service, you can meal prep, you can have someone else in your household make it, you can hire a professional chef... the list goes on. This is where we then start to look at the idea of consequences. You don't have to make dinner every night, let's look at the results if you do (you feel like you don't have time for anything else), or if you do not (maybe it costs a bit more money, maybe your partner is a terrible cook) and decide which results you are okay with.

Chapter 19: Should (the dreaded "S" word)

Bring the past, only if you are going to build from it.
Dominick Estrada

I want you to think back to yesterday. How many times did you say "should" to yourself? I would have a hard time believing it was none, but it may have been as few as one time and as many as one hundred times. "Should" is one of those comma words. You know the ones; you use it so often it's almost unnoticeable.

We overachievers—anxiety-ridden, history-thinking folks that we are—re-hash our choices, our words, and our actions many times before coming to grips with them. "Should" is one of the words we use to do that. "Should" keeps us stuck in our unrealistic expectations, our little "t" truths, our failures. "Should" is a word that that lies to us. It tells us that we are not quite good enough. Ugh. That feels gross to even write. But that is what it says. "Should" has a lot of power in our anxious mind. One of the ways to gain control over our anxious mind is to learn to think about things in a new way.

Should. (Good God, y'all.) What is it good for? (Absolutely Nothing, Sing it again.)

Ideally "should" would help us understand right and wrong. I should eat vegetables. I shouldn't give meth to children. Right? No guilt, no shame, just leaning closer to the black or white and helping us make decisions.

What happens in our anxious brain? "Should" becomes the big, fat, dividing line between black and white and indicates if you do something on one side (because you shouldn't), you are bad. Or if you do something and realize you should have done something else, you are bad. "Should" becomes a way to determine if we are okay or not. And that's not okay!

Are there areas in which we should have done something different? Maybe. Every situation is different. It is important to change the question from "Should I have?" to "Did I make an intentional choice?" If we made that choice non-judgmentally, fully present, and on purpose, well then, it was the best choice we could make with the information we had. This means we can stop beating ourselves up over the decision we made. If we doubt and struggle and flop through the decision-making process, maybe we need to stop and practice our S.O.B.E.R. skills instead of waiting to guilt ourselves later with a "should."

Dr. Albert Ellis had a quaint saying of "Stop shoulding on yourself." And I love it. Because it gives a visual image doesn't it? If you are shoulding on yourself you are not taking care of yourself, showing self-love, and filling your own cup. Which is problematic if you want to live your best life. I often use the statement of "you used the 'S' word" in my therapy with people to help them catch how often they are shoulding on themselves.

So how do we stop shoulding on ourselves?

Step one: Notice. Have a little tracker on your phone, keep a pad and pencil with you and track how many times you say or think that you should or shouldn't have. These could be statements like "I should be better by now." "I should be able to do this." "I should have chosen the other lunch." "I should be a better friend." "I shouldn't eat this whole cake." Tracking helps us to understand the extent of the intensity of the behavior.

Step two: Stop it! (That will be $5.) The first step of S.O.B.E.R. is to stop once you have noticed the behavior or the need to make a decision. It's not so easy to just stop it, but it is the next step. You need to catch yourself in the act and make a different choice. Stop and observe. Take your five breaths and decide how to move forward, without judgment, fully present, and on purpose. Most often when you are making intentional choices you are not going to choose to should on yourself with reckless abandon! You are going to make the best choice you can with the information you have.

You can also use these other reframing thoughts to help you make these decisions:

- Is this statement and a big "T" truth?
- Would you tell your friend this same "should" statement?
- What would I like to have happen instead of what do I think should have happened?
- Is taking time to focus on this helping me achieve my goals?
- Is focusing on this helping me to feel the way I want to feel?

As you start noticing, putting things in perspective, and making new choices, you will notice that you should on yourself less and less. That is very freeing.

Chapter 20: Whose Stuff is this?

> Growth is painful, change is painful, but nothing is as painful as staying stuck where you don't belong.
>
> *Mandy Hale*

As a psychologist, I often ask the question, "Whose stuff is this?" when people carry the weight of their spouse, their boss, the stranger in the grocery store, when they are feeling anxious about another's thoughts or feelings. When they are taking responsibility for another's actions because they wanted everything to turn out okay. When they want to shield others from bad news, pain, uncomfortable feelings. I ask this question when I can recognize that the person is taking responsibility for another person's actions or feelings, and they don't need to.

We are not the police of others. We are not responsible for others. We are only responsible for ourselves. This doesn't mean we don't care about other people (clearly, we do!), but we don't have to carry it for them. We can help them carry it if it is an intentional choice. One of the ways we can make sure it is an intentional choice is by getting in the habit of asking ourselves, "Whose stuff is this?" If it is mine, "What am I going to do about it?" If it is theirs, "I need to let it go." They need to be responsible for it. If they want help, they can ask. If they want help and don't ask, is it going to be best for me to offer or to ask and give them an opportunity to tell me what they need?

My husband is amazing. He can look at my face—I think I have a poker face but clearly not with him—and know when I have a question, a need, or a desire. He gives me plenty of space to ask for what I need. He also knows that when I get too far in my independent, overachiever mode I won't ask for what I need and then I will get angsty and frustrated. That is usually when he knows to ask me what I need. He also knows that "nothing" is not the truthful answer most of the time. He gives me enough room that if I want to sit around and be angsty because I don't want to ask for help or get what I need, that's my stuff. He is patient and kind and gives me room to sit with my really uncomfortable feelings. (You know the ones where you really hope this uncomfortable feeling is indigestion but you know it is emotional and there isn't a release that will be really all that helpful except dealing with it? Ugh!)

By allowing me my stuff he is actually giving me a great gift of opportunity to grow. It's not his job to make me grow or even to really help me grow. He joined in on this circus act because he loves me and being a part of my growth is a byproduct of that. I love that he gives me the room to grow.

If you are unsure if you are taking on other people's responsibilities, or unsure if this is causing difficulty in your life, ask yourself these questions; ask yourself these questions when you are at a place of really struggling to navigate your emotions:

- Do you feel unsatisfied?
- Are you are convinced you should just do everything yourself?
- Are you feeling bogged down by other people's problems?
- Are you going above and beyond all the time for someone, everyone, anyone?

There is a difference between global codependency and kindness. Kindness doesn't feel heavy. When you offer to walk an old lady across the street, offer to help a mom with six kids trying to move her cart to the parking lot, or pick up a toy a child has dropped, it does not feel like a burden. You don't carry that around all day and feel the weight of the world. Kindness is light, momentary, and thoughtful. Global codependency, overachieving, and people-pleasing feel heavy. You feel the burden, you think on it a lot, you stress about it. You fret about doing the right thing, about how others will think of you, about what will be lost or gained at this moment. When was the last time you had those thoughts about helping an old lady cross the street? Heavy—not heavy?

Chapter 20: Whose Stuff is this?

One way to test if you are acting out of kindness or out of a need to please others is to look back at your actions. If you were acting out of kindness, you will probably look back with a sense of contentment for having helped. If you are acting from a need to please others you will more likely question if you did enough.

It is important to learn to ask yourself, "Whose stuff is this?" To help determine if this stuff is your stuff, ask yourself these questions:

- If I make the decision/choice to do this, how is it helping me grow?
- Is it hindering me from moving forward?
- Is there something else I could be doing to give myself room to grow?
- What is the benefit of doing this?
- Once you have identified stuff that is not yours, here are some questions to figure out what to do with this extra stuff:
- If it is not my stuff, how can I give it back?
- What is my obligation with this?
- How can I communicate with this person about the ownership of this decision?

Chapter 21: Living Intentionally

Realize deeply that the present moment is all you ever have.
Eckhart Tolle

There are three components of living intentionally. These are the three bullet points from our S.O.B.E.R. skills: non-judgmentally, fully present, and on purpose. These concepts are more than just a way to gauge if your decision is the right one for you in the moment. They are a way to help you navigate everyday life.

Fully Present. I clearly remember my parents saying, "You can't concentrate on homework while listening to music or watching TV." Now, I love a good multitask and have been watching TV or listening to music while doing homework for many years of my life. Truth is I can do them both, but I am not being fully present or purposeful with either. One skill we learn as psychologists is to be fully present for our clients, not thinking of our grocery list, not paying attention to our phones or smart watches when they beep. Not wondering who is doing what in the lobby. Just being present for our person. For us multitaskers that is *hard*. It is tough to slow everything down and just be present.

Remember when you were learning to drive and your parents (grandparents, aunt/uncle or whoever) told you to turn off the radio and focus? Same thing. When we are being intentional, we are turning off our distractions. We are focused on what we are doing, choosing, and saying.

When I think of intentional living I think of living in the present. Not focusing on what is coming, not worrying about what has happened, not wishing for something different, not thinking about what isn't. Just being here. Then I apply one of my favorite ideas, "Love it or change it." If I am in a space that is cold, I either love it (relishing the crispness and being fully present in it), or I change it (I get a sweater, blanket, do some jumping jacks, rub my hands together, or leave.) If I can't change the situation, I can still change my perspective by doing some reframing and learning how to love it.

Although we can change (or work to change) most things in life, some changes are not quick or not practical. How much other people recycle, gravity, or the existence of weird green vegetables (you know who you are broccoli) aren't easily changed. We can't always change external circumstances, no matter how hard we work at it, but we don't always have to. We also have the option of changing our mindset and perspective which can change the way we feel about the situation.

I think about this a lot with people. I can't change others. I could tell them to do things differently, I could ask them to change, but I can't actually make them change. So that gives me options. Love it/them for who they are and what they bring to the table. Or change it/me/them. Ask for things to be different, change my own feelings about it, or change being with them.

By living intentionally, we can get to a place where we cast out thoughts like "this always happens to me," "the world is out to get me," or "there are somethings we can't do anything about." You can stop living on autopilot and get back in the driver's seat again. We live in an era where you can automate a lot of things (I just recently set up Alexa in my home), but automation and living on autopilot are two different things. One may make our life easier by setting up routines or facilitating our daily activities. The other means we are skipping through actual experiences. When was the last time you focused on each tooth while you were brushing it? Now I am not one for being so mindfully focused that I spend two minutes caressing each tooth, but when I focus on these mundane activities and really try to live them intentionally, I notice that my teeth feel cleaner. I remember why I am brushing my teeth, not just because it is part of my routine, but because it keeps me healthy and that is important to me (and every six months my dental hygienist reminds me that I only have to floss the teeth I want to keep). I make conscious decisions about how long I actually brush before bed instead of a quick once over just because it is part of my routine. The same thing goes with eating, drinking, talking with friends, driving, shopping—anything. As we practice living intentionally everything gets put in perspective. We don't have to worry about the past, because we made our choices non-judgmentally, fully present, and on purpose. We have nothing to worry over.

Now some of you are saying, "But Tara, what if I realize later I did make the wrong choice, because there *was* a wrong choice!" (I hear it in your voice; you are still struggling with the idea of black-and-white thinking.)

When I help clients with this in therapy, I take on the role of an archeologist. I ask question after question to start gently brushing away all of the irrelevant material (dirt) that is covering up the real thought or worry. Here are some of the questions I often use to do this: What if you did make the "wrong" choice? How "wrong" was the choice? What do you mean by "wrong"? Are you just afraid it was "wrong", or was it really? Can you change the choice? Is there something you can do? Was that choice really life or death, or was it just a choice you wish you could have done differently? It's okay to wish you had done something differently, I do; but wishing you had done it differently is not the same as having made the wrong choice. It also does not mean you can't work to change the results, but if you are spending all your energy focusing on why it was wrong, you won't have any energy left for changing the result with your next choice. Use your S.O.B.E.R. skills and decide what you want to do about it now and make new choices.

Non-Judgmental. When I explain S.O.B.E.R. to people I always ask, "What part of this is going to be the hardest for you?" Folks who self-describe as perfectionistic, overachievers, and guilt/shame hoarders tend to say "Non-judgmental."

Non-judgmental is a difficult thing. Our brains are wired to put things in boxes. If I say a four-legged furry animal, what do you think of? I was thinking of a cow. Did you think dog or cat? Or, heck, there are some furry pigs! I gave you a box and we came up with several sub-boxes. We teach kids to discriminate between different things with different features. We teach them to judge things by fitting them into categories. This form of judgment is really making an assessment based on finding common attributes. Any four-legged, furry animal would have fit in the box. As we grow up though, we learn to use the idea of judgmental and apply it to right and wrong not as an assessment, but as a moral or ethical judgment. We say right and wrong, but we mean good and bad. We are funny little creatures.

Non-judgmental doesn't mean that everything in the universe is okay. It applies more to how we talk to ourselves, how we set ourselves up for success (or failure), and how we apply our decisions to our lives. Think about the last time you saw someone and thought to yourself, "Wow that lady is fat." Now, when I put that in context with your values and who you want to be, does it fit? Do you want to be a person that comments on people's size like that? My guess is probably not. Now, when you look in the mirror and say, "Ugh, I'm so.... (fat, thin, ugly, etc.)" How is that different? You are still being judgmental and mean. That doesn't fit your values either.

There is an old saying about how you should treat others how you want to be treated. I'd like to add to that for all us Judgy-McJudgerson's, we should treat ourselves how we would treat others. Because we are worth loving, liking, and being kind to.

When we are non-judgmental and we are intentional with our choices, we have an opportunity to grow and learn. We are able to admit that we are not perfect (*gasp*) and we are in process. Being in process is a good thing because we don't have to know it all yet. We don't have anything to prove.

I know I lost many of you at this point. I mean, how do we get an "A" if we don't have a grading scale—even for ourselves? How will I know I am the best; how will I know that it is perfect? How will I be able to hold my head up around my spouse/partner/friend/parents/kids? Well...

Non-judgmental means I honor my choices as valid. It means I trust myself to make the best choices with what I have.

On-Purpose. I want you to grab 24 coins (and really you could use anything—poker chips, rocks, etc.). But whatever you choose grab 24 of them. Now I want you to grab some Post-it notes and start writing out on individual Post-it notes all the places you put time or energy in your life.

For example:

Sleep
Work
Eating
Time with friends
Reading (or whatever self-care you do)
Exercise
Time with family
Art
Volunteering
Cleaning

Just keep listing categories until everything is out there. Now spread them out on the table and start to put them in an order that makes sense to you. Recognize some may be weekly things (like mowing your lawn). If you find weekly things, pull them off to the side and just focus on the daily things.

Now, you are going to take your coins and place them according to the time you spend on those things, one for each hour of the day. So, if you need eight hours of sleep, move eight coins to the sleep Post-it note. If you need two hours exercising, move two coins. Here's an example of what that might look like:

8 hours of sleep
1 hour of exercise
1 hour of to-do list accomplishing
8 hours of work
2 hours commute
1 hour of eating
1 hour TV
1 hour of reading
+ 1 hour of shower/hygiene

---

24 hours

This means if I want to do other things, I need to make changes in my world. Simple as math. (If math is simple to you. It is not simple to me most of the time! That's why I have a husband for whom math is easy.) Once you have your plan, you can make adjustments purposefully. A few years ago, that one-hour exercise would have been a freebie hour, but I have built it in because it has become important to me. Design your day. Create room for the things that are most important for you. This could be learning a new hobby, or having an hour at a coffee shop before you go to work. Your day will be different than others. If you don't have room in your day to do the things that fill your cup, you won't be living your best life.

You need to budget your time. "Budget" feels like a harsh word, but budget is just a word. You need to be purposeful about how you budget your time. When you make a to-do list that is 100 things long on a day you have a 12-hour shift and you know you need eight hours sleep, you are likely not going to get that list done. When you have 50 things left on your list at the end of the day and start getting judgmental about your abilities, you find yourself going down a negative spiral. And by you, I mean me. This is a trap I have fallen into many times. Which is why I love my planner.

I have tried many planners over the years, and it took me a while to find one that really gave me the ability to make more on-purpose decisions about how I navigate my day. My favorite so far has vertical columns for the day that let me create a to-do list. Each month I go through and put things that are daily tasks on the to-do list, and then add to it for each day when I sit down with my honey-lemon water in the morning. When I was learning to be intentional, I added everything to my list from the previous day that I didn't get done and thought that was a great way for me to keep tasks moving forward. Pretty soon I had to start writing extra sticky notes to add to the list and got to the place I realized I was trying to do too many things in one day. I started to feel overwhelmed, frustrated, and like a failure, because I couldn't complete the list.

I was able to reduce my frustration and feelings of failure by learning the difference between important and time sensitive, important with no timeline, and not important but would love to someday. In school, I had a syllabus to tell me all the things that needed to be complete by the end of the semester. So I put it in my planner and got it done. Well, life doesn't have a semester's end! I ended up having things that just needed to get done, all the time, forever! The tool I had learned didn't work in my new situation. So I had to create my own to-do list and my own timeline. I had to figure out what things were important, what things were wishes, and what was going to be okay to skip. (Because, yes—it is okay to skip.) I traded in my pattern of moving things over to my next day list for an on-going list that is not in my planner. Things with actual timelines go in my planner and I make a plan to do them. My on-going list is for stuff I get to when I get to it.

If you have purposefully planned your day, and you still feel like there are important things you don't have time for it is okay to ask for help. Take a moment and think of someone you could ask to help. Having trouble thinking of a time you could ask for help? I am thinking about those times when you have to take work home with you and you clearly would rather do anything else but work when you are at home. Maybe ask your boss for tips on how to complete the amount of work you have at work. Don't just assume he knows that you are struggling. Work it out with her. Or if it feels like you are doing laundry 24/7, ask your partner, your kids, or reach out for other options to have someone help with this task. One of the things I know about us overachievers and perfectionists is we tend to believe that we need to do everything ourselves.

Chapter 22: Fight, Flight, or Freeze

Between stimulus and response there is a space. In that space is our power to choose our response.
Victor Frankl

One of my favorite topics to spend time on in therapy is the discovery of who we are. In order to do that I like to start with our initial response to a startling situation. It is described in psychology as the "fight, flight, or freeze response." I love using animals to describe it.

Fight animals tend to make me think of a bear lumbering at me with speeds I didn't think possible, and then standing on its hind legs bellowing up to the sky that he is big and scary and no one should mess with him. A snake also comes to mind with its coiling, hissing, and then the immediate jab at an enemy with its fangs. Animals that leap at you instead of away when they are scared.

Flight animals are the runners and flyers of the world. A loud sound and, *bam!* They are out of there. Birds, rabbits, and squirrels—all gone in a blink if you surprise them.

Freeze animals are the ones who just wait it out to see if you are dangerous: opossums, raccoons, cats. Opossums have a two-pronged approach to threats. First, they stare: "You think you are lucky, punk, well, do ya?" And, second, if you are a real threat, they just play dead.

We have an initial startle response that is automatic. There isn't a single response that is better than one of the others. All of them have purpose, and we need some of each of them in our world. If we were all fighters, there would be a heck of a lot of problems in the world solved by social and emotional aggression. If we were all flighters, we wouldn't solve much of anything; we would run away! If we were all freezers, we wouldn't get much done, would we? As individuals, I believe we have the ability to tap into any of them as we need to.

We tend to get caught up in our shame around how we respond—I'm too aggressive, not aggressive enough, I always get walked over, I just freeze up—but these responses are totally normal. Release that shame. Understand your natural instinct and start working on how you want to use that differently. Use your S.O.B.E.R. skills and be intentional about your responses. As we are able to be intentional about our responses, we can allow for the response to match the situation. S.O.B.E.R. doesn't have to take forever; it may take a fraction of a second to realize we need to jump into a fight that is happening, or a fraction of a second to recognize this isn't a scary thing. We will still have our instinctual reaction, but we get an amazing opportunity to not act on that feeling. When we take the time to choose our own responses to the situation, we don't have to feel shame about how we responded, because we made our choice intentionally.

I'm a freezer. I just want to wait and see what happens. I often describe myself as an opossum when it comes to conflict and stressful situations. Conflict is difficult for me to sit with; I want to check out until it is over. As a psychologist, I can't. Conflict is a part of my bread and butter. (I like to think of conflict as the annoying poppy seed in bread that gets stuck in your teeth until you deal with it!) So it is hard for me to avoid it. Over the years I have had to learn how to tune my opossum to hearing conflict, and deciding how involved I need to be in it. Is it important for the clients I see to navigate their own distress at this point, or do I need to go in and soothe? Is it important for me to regain control in this room before people get emotionally hurt? Or do I need to wait and gather further information? Any of these responses work as an actual answer, but taking time to think things through gives me the opportunity to respond to the situation in the way that will be best for the client—and honestly, best for me in the long run.

Chapter 23: You Are Only Committed Paycheck to Paycheck

> Your present circumstances don't determine where you can go; they merely determine where you start.
>
> *Nido Qubein*

My dad once told me, "You are only committed to this employer paycheck to paycheck." He went on to describe that my only agreement with them was to the work involved with this paycheck. Once I got the first paycheck, I was in a place to make a new agreement with them for the work associated with the next pay period. It was always up to me to make the agreement and agree to the terms of the new pay period. If you read that and thought, "Sacrilege!" then you know what I felt when I first heard this from my dad.

When he said, "You are only committed to this job paycheck to paycheck," my internal response was, "You don't understand. They need me. They won't find anyone else who can do what I am doing. They are already short staffed. They can't possibly survive. I can't leave them in a lurch. I told them I would stay for a couple of years. How could what he is saying be true?"

This is hard for us overachievers to understand. We feel like when we have made a commitment to something, we need to see it through.

I have seen women who desperately want to *not* have a baby shower have one because they already said "yes." Couples get married because they already told everyone they were. People go to events that they don't want to attend because they already committed to it. People stay in jobs because they feel like they have to.

They don't have to.

My perceptions and beliefs fueled my decision to stay longer than I needed to at that job. Did I learn cool stuff? Yep. Did I meet amazing people? Yep. Did it meet some needs for me? Yep. I have no regrets for how long I stayed. I don't play the "what if" game very often, but what if I had left when I first had the inkling? Would I have had different experiences? Yep. Better? Who knows? It is important to be intentional and thoughtful about the reasons you stick with any decision. It is okay to check in with yourself and reassess your choices and even change them if you want to.

The only thing that keeps us where we don't belong is our own over commitment to it. Would someone be disappointed if we quit? Would it be embarrassing? Would it be another big change? Would it be detrimental to the company or person? Would it cost a lot? Maybe. But staying is going to cost you too. Staying may be detrimental to you. Moving on may be a big change you can handle. It might be just the thing that is wonderful for your life.

One of the best tools for evaluating if you should stay somewhere is S.O.B.E.R. Each paycheck, anniversary, decision to say "yes" to a date, emotional check in about the wedding—stop. Observe: inside and out. And breathe. Examine the options (five of them!) and then respond with what you want to do. Do it non-judgmentally, fully present, and on purpose. If you purposely choose to stay at the job, make sure you are doing it because you have evaluated what is going on inside and outside of you.

Just because you agreed to something doesn't mean you have to stay with it forever. You can choose to move on from it when you are ready to make that new choice. It is important to continually embrace your ability to choose. Your choice is not good or bad, it is just a choice—a choice that, if you use S.O.B.E.R. skills, you will be confident in and be able to live with non-judgmentally.

Chapter 24: Batting Those Baby Blues

> We meet ourselves time and time again in a thousand disguises on the path of life.
>
> *Carl Jung*

One of my favorite stories growing up was the one my mom tells of a swimming lesson I took advantage of.[6] It has stayed with me and has been so applicable in therapy, in my choices, and in my development as a strong independent woman.

Let's set the scene: I was young—I'm not sure how old—but I was in swimming lessons learning to do the freestyle stroke. They explained that I was expected to be able to put my face in the water and turn my head and breathe by now. But I hated putting my face in and out of the water like that. When they told me to swim underwater, no problem. I had goggles on and was prepared for that! But the back and forth with no goggles and water spraying up my nose? Nope! So I pushed off the side, began the swim, and gave up and started fake flailing—you know, with a sad little "cough-cough" and the pathetic effort of moving my arms around. The instructor came over with the rescue stick and let me kick my legs and hold on to the rescue stick as I made my way across the pool. With a small grin, I got out of the pool.

---

6 Another story I really love from my childhood was the "I can make more of you" story. When my brother and I were young and did something we shouldn't—not really across the line but definitely "bad" as my parents saw it—my parents would tell the story that we "used" to have an older brother. And if we kept messing up then my parents could "get rid of us too" and just make more children. My brother and I were old enough to understand that this was not serious. We understood hyperbole at that age, even if we did not yet know the word. It sounds a little horrible to put in my book, but it is one of my favorite stories. That threat that wasn't a threat but was just enough a threat to keep us in line.

When my mom tells the story, she says she collected me and told me this: If you can bat your baby blues and get someone to do something for you, that's great. But you best be able to do it yourself.

I broke down on the freeway in South Central LA at 2:30 in the morning with a girlfriend from college with a flat tire. Oh my gosh. This was the kind of moment my mom was talking about. I damn well better be able to change my own tire! I can't just hope some passerby is going to take care of that! I can't just call a tow truck (it was before cell phones were really a thing) and the call box was over two miles away! I did know how to change my tire and got in there and took care of business. Got off that freeway and worked it out.

My battery died at a gas station outside of a Fred Meyer in Newberg. As I was pushing my car away from the pump to get it out of the way, the guy behind me jumped out of his car and helped me push mine to the side. He said, "If you run in and get a battery for your car, I'll wait for you and install it." So I did. He waited and installed the battery and made my day! I didn't have to get my hands dirty, call a tow truck, or take any extra time out of my day. Baby blues, check!

I have wrestled with both sides of the "help" problem, from "I can't ask for help"—because I don't deserve it, should be able to do it on my own perspective—to "someone should do this for me because I am always doing something for other people," or the "I can't do this on my own" perspective. It has been a long journey to recognize that I am a grown woman with the ability to do anything I put my mind to and can also ask for help or get other people to take care of things for me if I choose. It has taken me a lot of work to get comfortable with this statement.

Chapter 25: Walking the middle path

Sophrosyne (n): a healthy state of mind, characterized by self-control, moderation, and a deep awareness of one's true self, and resulting in true happiness.

One of my favorite tools in Dialectical Behavioral Therapy is finding the "wise mind." The wise mind is the balance between the emotional mind and the rational mind. Finding the wise mind is another way to help make sure we are finding that middle ground and not making extreme choices.

The rational mind comes across as cold, logical, fact-driven, focused, built upon logic and science, and experiments without bias. On the other side, the emotional mind comes across as hot, irrational, quick to act, gut instinct, scattered, reactive, experiencing emotional highs and lows.

The wise mind finds the place where these two overlap. It gives us the opportunity to feel passionately and choose a response appropriate to the situation.[7] It allows us to be warm to what is happening, not cold or hot. It allows us to have a hunch and work out a system to decide if it is right or wrong. It is not black and white this wise mind—it is grey.

See why I like it so much? It sounds a lot like living in the grey area.

Learning to use our wise mind helps us do a better job with our S.O.B.E.R. skills. It is hard to truly feel non-judgmental down the road if we have not taken into account both our logic and our emo-

---

7 My husband explains this in his classes as "You can't have the Enterprise without both Spock and Kirk."

tions. Too much of one, too little of the other—in either direction—and we tend to regret our decisions.

So walking the middle path, staying in the grey, roping in the rational and emotional sides of our brains gives us the most balanced perspective that is likely closer to the truth.

I think (and our anxiety tries to keep it this way) we are often taught to try to be more rational and put less emphasis on our emotions. Yep. Talking to you, reader. Most of you aren't letting your emotions run your life. Most of you are really good at putting those emotions in a closet in your soul and locking it and then locking the door to that room and then pretending like it doesn't exist. Am I right? Some of you have even gone to the extent of walling off that door and hoping no one asks why there isn't another bedroom in your house. You know who you are.

We use phrases like "it's fine," "no problem," or "no worries." Those quick, almost automatic responses say, "Nothing to see here." These are often indicators that there is more going on than you recognize. You might not even notice that you are doing it. How often do you check in with yourself about whether you really have feelings about something? More often I would guess that you are busy trying to make sure you aren't an imposition. That you aren't causing problems. That you are being amenable. You follow the "rules" because that is how you earn a gold star; that is logical.

Once you have identified those phrases that tell you there might be more going on, you need to give yourself an opportunity to check in when you say them. If you are quick to say "no worries," every time you catch yourself saying it make an intentional effort to check in using S.O.B.E.R. Ask yourself, "Is this really okay? Do I have a feeling about how this should go one way or another? Do I have an opinion? What would I share if there was a guarantee that there would be no repercussions? If I could ask for anything to change in this moment what would it be?" If the answer is "nothing"—great. "No worries" it is and keep moving. If you do have feelings about it, lean into those feelings. Think about what your emotions are saying, share your feelings, ask for what you need, change direction.

Good partners, friends, teachers, strangers, will let you change your mind, hear you out, and be okay with it. Sometimes people will get frustrated, mean or rude. But that's okay. You are okay. You have worth, and your feelings have worth as well. You will be enough with or without their acceptance of your change of plan or your different desire.

Chapter 26: Values

Who looks outside, dreams; Who looks inside, awakes.

Carl Jung

When we are making decisions that are non-judgmental, we can reduce the chances of feeling guilt or shame later on. How do we know what we will not be judgmental about later though? This is where knowing our core values comes in.

So what are core values and how do you identify yours? Values are the themes in which you live your life. You know when you are not living them because everything just seems to be out of whack. You can't get things done in time, you miss important deadlines, things are out of place, and your relationships suffer. Your values help you take your choices and put them into perspective.

Values are the North Star of your soul. They always point you in the right direction to feel settled and at home. Does this mean you can't try new things and explore? Nope. You absolutely can try new things! When you do you will figure out if those new explorations match your values.

For many years now I have lived in the middle of Oregon wine country. I joke at times with my friends in the wine community who say, "Wine is an acquired taste." I tell them I don't want to spend time acquiring a taste—I want it to taste good the first time! But I know that is just my impatience. There are some things you will want to build into your life that you don't love the first time around, but that help you meet a value. I never feel better than when I have worked out in the morning. (Mostly because my watch gives me a gold star.) Over the course of the rest of the day, I know that I have met a goal and I am going to crush it all day long. Do I like working out? Not really. I would much rather sit on the couch with a book near the fireplace, but exercise does make a difference in my attitude the rest of the day. And that is because it meets a core value. Achievement is one of my core values. When I set a goal and meet that goal it sets me up to have a good day.

So here's a small list of core values (there are many more):

Family
Health
Money
Fame
Vulnerability
Service to others
Being loved
Ecology
Fairness
Hope

The activity I do in therapy is to take a deck of Values Cards (about 85 of them in total) and have clients sort them into two piles: important and not important. We weed out as many as we feel like in that first sort and set them aside. We then pull the important pile and separate those into two piles: important and very important. This is where the good, hard work comes in. This section is hard because everything feels important. But when we get the opportunity to compare two values it does become pretty obvious which values really touch our soul. As we pull together these lists, we start talking about each value and discovering which values are really ours—and which values were bestowed upon us.

I feel like I was given the value of hard work from my parents. I'm not sure it is actually a value of mine; maybe the value of mine is wanting to be known for doing hard work. Actually, just to be known maybe. The value of hard work was bestowed upon me. It is a value I would choose from the pile, but when I have spare time on my hands, hard work isn't the first thing that comes to mind. I just want to sit and relax. A value of mine is more likely leisure. Do I do the hard work and feel good about it? Yeah! I love to feel like a badass when I have done a million things or done something it should have taken two people to do and I did it by myself! This hits the value of accomplishment, but if I could have the accomplishment without the hard work, I think I would be just as happy.

Core values help us make decisions. They keep us on track when we are thinking of changing course, not because we shouldn't try new things, but because we need to make sure what we are trying is going in the direction we should go. When we make decisions intentionally using S.O.B.E.R. skills we notice that they line right up with our core values, and then it does feel like things are going the way they should.

Our values are that North Star we are aiming at with every choice we make. When we are making decisions that do not keep us aiming at our values, we might notice that it is harder to make choices non-judgmentally. We may be off course. This is the time to review our values and to make sure that they are our values.

One of the key elements we work at in this activity is sorting the cards to make sure that the values my clients pick are their own with no guilt or shame. Many times, folks leave the family card in their most important pile. And as we dig deeper, they realize they think it should be most important (did you catch that "S" word? I sure did!). *Should* be? Why? Who says? Does it mean you are a bad person if family is not your most important value? Why? Who says? It is one hundred percent okay for family to not be your most important value. You can still love and value and cherish them; these ideas are not mutually exclusive.

Ecology is not one of my core values, yet I recycle. World peace is not in my core values, and yet I pray for peace and support causes and people who strive for it. When we start tackling these "should" statements, we find that there are underlying core beliefs that must be addressed. In Cognitive Behavioral Therapy one of the key elements to making lasting change is to address the core beliefs that have been built up and supported by our actions.

So what's the difference between core beliefs and core values? Great question! Glad you asked!

Core values, to keep with the metaphor of the North Star, are the guiding principles that echo the deepest elements of what makes us individuals. They are the culmination of what makes us "us." No one else has the same set of core values in the way that we do. Could they sort the cards the same way in my office? Sure, but for different reasons, in a different order, or to meet a different need. When we live our core values, our soul feels settled. Our life feels more like it is going in the way it is supposed to go.

If core values give us our direction, core beliefs are more like the stories we tell ourselves or have been told to help us make sense of the world around us. They tell us why we should go in that direction. I'm envisioning a campfire and elders sharing how the world became, and what our destiny is.

You have heard the story: A kid has been told he will never amount to anything and ends up on the streets because he feels like he had no other destiny. He accepted the story he heard and did not feel like he could change it.

Or the opposite story: A kid being told she will never amount to anything who then goes on to build a Fortune 500 company and prove the world wrong. That is someone who didn't believe the story and changed it. The situation was the same, but one challenged the story they were told. Sometimes the story is based in truth and sometimes it is based on a distortion. It is up to us to recognize this and choose which stories to believe.

When we form our beliefs, we are writing a little "t" truth story to tell us why we should make the choices we do. It is important to examine these stories often to make sure we still feel that they hold true with our big "T" truths of the core values we are aiming at.

Chapter 27: Being Vulnerable

> There is a sacredness in tears. They are not the mark of weakness, but of power. They speak more eloquently than ten thousand tongues. They are the messengers of overwhelming grief, of deep contrition and of unspeakable love.
>
> *Washington Irving*

For many years of my life, school was difficult for me because I was always worried that I didn't know the right answer. Actually, it was not just school, life was difficult for me because I felt the expectation to know everything, to be able to answer any question. If someone asked me how much a shirt cost in a store, I would get flustered and anxious because I didn't know and felt I should. If someone asked a question about why the sky was blue and not purple—ahh! Terrifying. I was always walking the path of "I best be able to do it myself," which means I should already know the answer (the far side of the bell curve) so I shouldn't ask any questions! Which is a total bastardization of what my mom meant when she talked about "batting my baby blues"!

I felt that asking questions was bad because it would just make me look dumb—until I met Christine. We went on a camping trip together with our boyfriends at the time (she married hers, I didn't). Along the trail, she would ask all sorts of questions. It was the first time I saw curiosity as something beautiful. In fact, it was the first time I even saw asking questions as okay. It didn't seem stupid at all to ask what kind of tree that was or what squirrels do in winter when they can't be out looking for food. Did they hibernate like bears? What is the best way to use the camp toilet? Is there a good way to sleep on this rocky terrain? I never would have asked those questions (or had the answers to them) without Christine. Christine gave me a real-life opportunity to see what vulnerability in knowledge was like. As an overachiever, one would think we are grossly curious beings, that we want to know all sorts of things and thus spend lots of time learning them. And that may be true for many overachievers—and for some it is more about looking like we know it, looking like we understand it, or just seeming competent enough to not look stupid. Ugh. That hits home.

If Christine had not asked those questions, I would have watched what everyone else did and made my best guess about how to copy them. I also would have been worried every moment that someone would notice that I was not doing it right, or if I was doing it right, that someone would ask me for help and I would need to have an answer for them.

Even though she did not know it (and still might not), Christine showed me that it is okay to not know everything. That being vulnerable can make you look intelligent. She showed me that I could learn new things as I go.

Seeing someone else have success being vulnerable let me know it was possible, it did not mean learning to do this for myself was a quick or easy transition. It has helped me to have some ways to reframe my thoughts so I could practice this in day-to-day life. Not knowing, not being able to, not being good at—these are all little "t" truths. These little "t" truths make vulnerability uncomfortable because they feel permanent. It is important to remember that they may be little "t" true in the moment, but they do not have to stay that way. One of the skills we need to increase our comfortability with being vulnerable is adding the word *yet* to our vocabulary. Transitioning from "I don't know this" to "I don't know this, yet" can help us change our perspective. It helps us move our little "t" truths from feeling permanent to being changeable.

Being changeable is a good start, but making the change is another thing altogether. To make a change we need another skill; we need to be willing to practice. Or as my anxiety translates: we need to be willing to fail at it several times until we get it right. That is tough. This takes us back to the idea that if something is hard, we must be doing it wrong, but that's not usually it. It is more likely we are using muscles that we have not used before or haven't used very much. Building mastery is hard because we do have to fail, admit we don't get something, or show vulnerability.

I don't know how to play chess. My husband loves chess. I believe he wishes I played. He has tried to teach me a few times and each time I give up and "don't want to learn." I think the real reason I don't want to learn is that I have a little "t" truth that I won't ever be as good as him (actually read my anxious voice saying he will be disappointed in my ability to play). Therefore, I will lose constantly and all that will show—again with a full burst of anxiety—is that I am not actually smart, I am not actually good enough for him. What if he realizes that and decides to leave me? (Anyone else follow that train of logic? Straight from Anxiety Town into the worst-case scenario swamp—like the fire swamp only there are no R.O.U.S.'s). Big "T" truth? He would love to have me learn to play chess and play with him on occasion. He would not be disappointed if I lost, and rather than think I am dumb, he would point out my improvement. My chess abilities were never a factor in our relationship. He knows just how smart I am and accepts that I don't play chess. Hard big "T" truth to swallow sometimes, but knowing the truth I can slow down that train and put it back on track. If I wanted to learn to play, I could and my husband would support me. In other words: I don't play chess, yet.

Chapter 28: Everybody Needs A Therapist

> Mental pain is less dramatic than physical pain, but it is more common and also more hard to bear. The frequent attempt to conceal mental pain increases the burden: it is easier to say "My tooth is aching" than to say "My heart is broken."
>
> *C.S. Lewis*

Who do you go to when you have a broken arm or are having heart palpitations? Who do you go to for your annual checkups? (Yes, you need to do those.) You go to the doctor. You check in, they look you over, they give you a diagnosis, and then you follow their directions and you get better. Makes total sense.

Who do you go to when you have anxiety, depression, manic symptoms or are just overwhelmed? Obvious. You go see your therapist. You have one, right? Everyone should. Having a long-standing relationship with a therapist can help you navigate life's problems.

Therapists can help you understand what types of things are normal, abnormal, or clinically significant. They can help you find a way to navigate the stresses of life. They help you identify problem systems or rhythms in your world. They can help you make decisions by helping you think through issues that come up. They can be there for you to make sure you are taking care of yourself and doing what is good for you.

Therapists aren't just people you spill your week to. They are people who help you to navigate the world differently. They give you space to feel the big feelings that sometimes are more of a struggle than we want to admit. They are the people who are focused solely on helping you make the decisions that are best for you.

Think about it: You go to a therapist who helps you navigate some anxiety. A year or so later you are struggling with the loss of a good friend. You call your therapist, and in your next session you discuss your grief and your loss. You work with them for a while and then launch into the next phase of your life. How awesome would it be to know that you have someone who is always there for you to help deal with the stuff that comes up, just like your primary care doc?

Couples should think about this too. Getting involved with a couple's therapist early on in a relationship can help you navigate concerns and develop good patterns. Keep that therapist around so that when something does come up you can just say, "Let's go see Bob." And both of you know Bob. Bob is not scary. It's not a big deal to say let's get some counseling—it's Bob. You have been with Bob for years so it's easy to say, "Let's see him so we can get this worked out." Seeing Bob does not mean something is wrong with your relationship; it may mean you want your relationship to be the best it can be.

If everyone had a therapist like they have a primary care doctor the stigma of mental health issues would be almost nonexistent. When was the last time someone said, "Wait, you have a Dentist? That's weird. Must mean there is something wrong." Uhm, never. People going to a doctor or a dentist *may* mean something is wrong, but it also may mean that nothing is wrong and you are just getting a checkup.

Having a therapist may mean something is going on right now that you need help with, or it may mean you are checking to see if anything is wrong. Either way, it is vital that you have the right person to help you with the right tasks.

For instance, my gynecologist may listen to my heart during an exam, but if she hears something funny, she is going to refer me to a heart specialist. My primary doctor may ask me about my sexual health and if something is up, she will refer me to my gynecologist. When I have a broken arm, though, I am not going to go to my gynecologist.

Explaining mental health as if it were a physical symptom might help people understand that it is not a choice. We don't choose to have a broken leg; sometimes it just happens. When it does, we go see a doctor to help us. It is not a choice to have crippling anxiety. We confuse mental health with a choice or a behavior because we can't see it. When we see someone with a broken leg we understand. We give them some space, open doors for them, and support them. We don't ask them to run a marathon. We don't usually see the markers of anxiety and depression on people so we ask them to do all the things they normally do and then struggle to understand why they can't. We discuss with them quick and easy tips to deal with it, and then get frustrated when they won't make the right "choices." It sucks to have people ask you to do things you can't. It sucks to disappoint them, disappoint yourself, and struggle with your own confidence and ability. There are a lot of challenges to having a mental health issue and living your life. That is why having a therapist can help. A therapist allows you to have someone in your corner all the time who can help you navigate the issues that come up.

Understanding the difference between having a broken leg and learning how to best navigate our world with a broken leg is important. It is also important to recognize that, although having a broken leg helps define how we act, it does not define who we are. We would say, "I have a broken leg," not "I am a broken leg." Our anxiety, our depression, or any other diagnosis does not define who we are, it puts a name to symptoms so we can better understand how to navigate life with those symptoms. It is easy to feel like these labels define us, and force us into or away from certain actions. "My anxiety kept me from..." "My depression doesn't let me..." But the truth is, we do still have choices. My anxiety may make that choice harder, or I may have to learn new ways to do the same thing because I feel depressed, but the choices are still ours.

Making choices in a way that best fits our circumstances, that allows us to move through life with less shame, with more power in our own lives, and most importantly with the understanding that we have worth—that is ultimately what this book is about.

Chapter 29: Worth

> Have patience with all things, but first yourself. Never confuse your mistakes with your value as a human being. You are perfectly valuable, creative, worthwhile person simply because you exist. And no amount of triumphs and tribulations can ever change that. Unconditional self-acceptance is the core of a peaceful mind.
>
> *Saint Frances de Sales*

We have talked a lot about worth throughout this book. The idea that you have worth just the way you are. You have nothing to prove, no one to impress. It's just you—and you are great. You have worth just because you exist.

In my practice, I challenge clients to come up with definitions of *value* and *worth*. Usually they compare them saying that value is what we put on something, and worth is what it is actually... um... worth. We laugh and talk about how hard worth is to define. We know what it means, until we try to apply it to ourselves. I tell a client—or I tell you, right now reader, in this book—that you have worth. You are *worthy*. You are quick to dismiss me because you don't see your value. But I'm not talking value—what you bring to the table, or what you can do, or what you are good at—I am just talking worth. Worth doesn't change. You have worth. Right here and now. Big "T" truth.

Amy Wolf, founder of the "don't give up signs" movement (www.dontgiveupsigns.com) was so kind to give me a little interview about value and worth. Amy shared her story about why she started the movement, and several of the ideas we talked about really stood out. She has printed these messages on cards to hand out to others, on yard signs, on postcards and bracelets:

- You matter
- Don't give up

- Your mistakes do not define you
- You are worthy of love

And more, but you can see the theme. You have worth. Sometimes you need others around you to help pull you through, but that does not change your worth. Sometimes we feel like giving up or we do give up, but we still matter. Sometimes we make mistakes (some big, and some small), but these do not tell us who we are, they do not define our worth.

As we wrote back and forth, I realized how much we were talking about the grey area in life, and about black and white. Sometimes we are strong, sometimes weak. Sometimes we are okay on our own, sometimes we need some support. Sometimes things go well and sometimes they do not. Life is made up of grey areas. And that is a *truth*. So much of life is in the grey areas. There are some things that I want you to walk away with at the end of this journey that are worthy of being labeled "big 'T' truths." Things that fall completely in the black and white.

You have worth. You matter.

You are on a journey to become your best self. Hopefully, some of the skills you learned in this book will help you get there. Take a step back from the black and white and live in the grey 96 percent of the time. Use your S.O.B.E.R. skills, practice them, and be intentional about the choices you make. You can do this.

Appendix A: The "I do not think this means what you think this means" word list

Brokenness

Definition: to be reduced to fragments; fragmented

How we often use it: Not good enough, not able to continue on, unusable

More realistic way of thinking about it: Not how we were when we started, this isn't a judgment of good or bad, it just means we have been affected by a part of life.

Budget

Definition: a plan for the coordination of resources and expenditures

How we often use it: Budget is a limiting word; it makes us feel like we are being deprived

More realistic way of thinking about it: Budgeting is a planning word; it allows us to make more intentional choices about how we use our time and resources.

Consequences

Definition: a result or effect, typically one that is unwelcome or unpleasant

How we often use it: The negative outcome of something.

More realistic way of thinking about it: This is more about just understanding that it is the end of a chain of events. Actions produce results.

Failure

Definition: lack of success

How we often use it: Failure is final. There is no other option.

More realistic way of thinking about it: Failure is just an opportunity to learn something. It gives us a chance to decide where we put our efforts.

Selfish

Definition: devoted to or caring only for oneself; concerned primarily with one's own interests, benefits, welfare, etc., regardless of others

How we often use it: Any time we are taking care of ourselves, any time we are not sacrificing ourselves for others.

More realistic way of thinking about it: Taking care of yourself allows you to take better care of the people around you. Taking care of yourself is not selfish. You are just as worthy and deserving of care as the people around you. It is okay to do that for yourself.

Selflessness

Definition: having little or no concern for oneself, especially with regard to fame, position, money, etc.

How we often use it: The ideal way to live your life and requires sacrificing yourself for others

More realistic way of thinking about it: Selflessness is one extreme—a more moderate version of selflessness lets you value helping other people while still taking care of yourself.

Should

Definition: used to indicate obligation, duty, or correctness, typically when criticizing someone's actions, used to indicate what is probable.

How we often use it: Things that don't live up to expectations I believe or I hold are wrong or bad. They encourage guilt and shame and feel like they are my responsibility to change or fix.

More realistic way of thinking about it: Should's job is to help us balance right and wrong decisions. It can help us identify when we are applying beliefs or expectations to something outside the true moral purpose of Should.

Appendix B: Breathing Exercises

Dragon Breathing

Pros: Really active process to breathing. Helps you focus on the activity and stay in the moment.

Cons: Not a great one to do in front of other people (looks a little intense!)

1. Sit comfortably
2. Place your hand out in front of you.
3. Close your index, middle, and ring finger, leaving your thumb and pinky out.
4. To begin the breathing exercise, hold one nostril shut with your thumb, breathe in for a count of 5.
5. Close the other nostril with your pinky and hold for a count of 5.
6. Release the nostril held by your thumb and breathe out for a count of 5.
7. Continue to breathe in and out using opposite fingers 5 times.

Square Breathing

1. Sit comfortably
2. Put your arm out in front of you and trace a square in the air.
3. As you go across the top breathe in for a count of 4.
4. As you go across the side breathe out for a count of 4.
5. As you go across the bottom breath in for a count of 4.
6. As you go across the side breathe out for a count of 4.
7. Continue to do this 5 times (or as many times as you like)

You can do this in many varieties, like tracing the sides of a piece of paper or your phone. You can trace a square on your leg or hand instead of in the air. Or you can rotate your foot in the shape of a square under your desk or while sitting on the couch.

Peaks and Valleys Breathing

1. Sit comfortably.
2. Take your non-dominant hand and spread your fingers out in front of you.
3. Take your dominant hand and begin tracing the sides of your fingers up each side (peak) and down each side (valley).
4. As you go up the peak breathe in for a count of 5.
5. As you go down the valley breath out for a count of 5.
6. Continue through all the peaks and valleys.
7. Repeat as desired

About the Author

Tara Sanderson, PsyD, MBA, would love to have an alphabet after her name. But something about student loans and needing to get on with life got in the way. But just in case you are interested in the letters she already has, Tara graduated *cum laude* with a bachelor's degree in Psychology from Vanguard University in Southern California. She received her doctorate in Clinical Psychology from George Fox University in Oregon, and her master's in Business Administration (Nonprofit Focus) from Marylhurst University in Oregon.

This is her first book and the culmination of one of her many dreams. Tara lives in Oregon with her husband and enjoys geocaching, photography, riding motorcycles, and saying things that make her husband roll his eyes and sigh.

Visit the author's Website at: www.drtarasanderson.com or connect with her on social media:

@drtarasanderson

Sign up for email updates on up-coming products and resources.

Text set in
Freight Sans Pro
and Freight Text Pro,
designed by Joshua Darden.
Type licensed through
Adobe Fonts.

CPSIA information can be obtained
at www.ICGtesting.com
Printed in the USA
FSHW011831250221
78944FS